Sylvia Bashline's
Savory Game Cookbook

Sylvia Bashline's Savory Game Cookbook

Sylvia G. Bashline

Stackpole Books

Published by
STACKPOLE BOOKS
Cameron and Kelker Streets
P. O. Box 1831
Harrisburg, PA 17105

Printed in the U.S.A.

Library of Congress Cataloging in Publication Data

Bashline, Sylvia G
  Sylvia Bashline's Savory game cookbook.

    1. Cookery (Game)   I. Title.   II. Title: Savory
game cookbook.
TX751.B27   1983   641.6'91   83-4730
ISBN 0-8117-2151-5   Ba

To Will Johns and Roger Latham, good friends who died
before their time.

Contents

Foreword

Some of the most treasured memories of my life are of those times spent in the company of Sylvia and Jim Bashline. Without exception, they are also fond memories of the finest game and fish meals.

It is not strange that the two—treasured personal memories and the fine game and fish meals—are one, for Sylvia and Jim Bashline have that rare ability of being able to marry the two better than any couple I know.

Though many of those events took place in the comfort and warmth of the Bashline home, many did not. I've watched them prepare game under some mighty unusual conditions, from lakeshore campfires, to deer camp ovens, to Coleman stoves perched on the tops of windy mountains. Others were on the tailgates of station wagons surrounded by breathtaking fall foliage or in pouring-down rains. Not only were the end products worth bronzing, but each was inevitably accompanied by an appropriate wine from the Bashline cellar.

Preparing and eating wild foods is not only a ritual with the Bashlines, it is a holistic experience. Indeed, the entire scenario of hunting and fishing is that way with those of us who try to do it right. We subscribe to the theory that anyone who picks up a rod or gun for the purpose of taking wild game or fish has automatically assumed at least four major responsibilities: to make a legal kill as efficiently as possible; to field-dress and protect the game against spoiling; to prepare the game, or have it prepared for eating, to the best of our ability; and to eat it. We believe that those who shirk any of these responsibilities are not true sportsmen.

Sylvia Bashline's Savory Game Cookbook was written for those of us who might not be as talented as Sylvia Bashline but who want to do it right. This book will give us as much pleasure preparing and eating our game as we had taking and caring for it.

There is no better teacher in the field of wild game preparation than Sylvia Bashline. Her recipes are all winners. They are easy to follow and rewarding to serve. I only wish I had a dollar for every time I have sat down to a superb wild-game dinner and then discovered that the recipe had originated with Sylvia Bashline. My monetary wealth would be exceeded only by my riches in having enjoyed her recipes—and her friendship.

George Harrison
Nature Editor, Sports Afield
Field Editor, National/International
Wildlife

Introduction

Sylvia Bashline's Savory Game Cookbook was written for people who would like to cook wild game but are afraid to try. It can be scary since game doesn't have all the fat that helps tenderize domestically grown animals.

Wild game does require specially designed recipes, but they need not be complicated. Game has such unique flavors that easy recipes are usually the best ones. With these recipes and good directions, someone who has never cooked wild game before can serve it with *confidence*. And that is what this book is all about; it's easier to do than you would ever dream.

Beginning game cooks need two other things besides easy recipes: they are common sense and a bit of good humor. The first has a big part to play in successful wild game cookery. I use a lot of butter, cream, wine, and fresh ingredients such as mushrooms in my recipes. However, I don't hesitate to substitute when an ingredient is not available in the boondocks or when a guest requires less salt, sugar, or cholesterol in his diet. Delicious meals can be concocted using margarine or cooking oil (instead of butter), evaporated or skim milk (instead of cream), fruit juices or beer (instead of wine) and *canned* mushrooms or other vegetables. Different herbs can be substituted for those listed in the recipes (use a light hand) or they can be omitted altogether in many cases. Game has so much natural flavor that it can often stand by itself. Use common sense and all will be well.

A sense of humor is also important. We all know cooks who, when the *smallest* thing goes wrong, do what I call the "cook's prance." They dwell on the mistake until all sitting at the table are tired of hearing that the sauce is lumpy, the soup curdled, the rolls are too brown, or the meat over done. Chances are, if a good, relaxed dinner atmosphere is maintained, no one will realize that the meal is less than perfect. And that's where the sense of humor comes in. Cooks should never take themselves too seriously. Cooking and eating the resulting meal should be fun—so relax, have a good time and *don't talk about little mistakes*.

It also helps to decide what type of a cook you are, gregarious or private. If you love to gab while cooking (my husband), let's hope you have a home with a large kitchen so guests can congregate there. On the other hand, if you are easily distracted and love to concentrate on the job at hand (me), enlist your spouse's cooperation to keep the kids and guests out of the kitchen.

Practice new recipes on the family first, if possible, and then take on guests. When entertaining, advance preparations can help cut down last minute kitchen time. Try to choose dishes that are easy in the last stages and you'll look like a hero.

Following this book will help you become a good game cook in a short time. I can't remember how much time it took me to discover that some game is great when served on the medium rare side—it was considerable. I think we all tend to start out over cooking food, and that includes vegetables, meats, and pastries. It's natural since you want it to be done. With game, some cooks seem to feel that since it doesn't come encased in plastic, fresh from the supermarket, that it isn't quite clean and that it must be *killed* again in the kitchen by cooking it to death. Another fallacy is that anything wild is gamey tasting. It isn't. It simply tastes like what it is, just like pork tastes like pork and chicken tastes like chicken. Don't try to hide the natural flavor of wild game, just enhance it.

In my opinion, most game cookbooks have too many recipes for each species. That makes it hard for readers to choose. And frankly, I don't think all of them are well tested. You'll find fewer game recipes in this book but each is guaranteed to satisfy.

Hopefully, that guarantee will encourage you to try more of the recipes. It's human nature to want to keep repeating a recipe that meets with approval. For instance, I know families that bag a deer almost every year, yet always prepare venison steak, Swiss-style. What a shame not to branch out when there are so many delicious ways to cook steak.

I want you to trust me: to experiment a bit with the recipes. Just because you haven't tried a cooking method before doesn't mean you can't tell if you'll like it. First check on the recipe notes in each section. They provide information on what type of bird or animal should be used, preparation time (vegetable chopping, meat frying, etc.—but not cooking time since that is in the recipe), and the general taste of the finished dish. Then, check the list of ingredients in the recipe. If your family is crazy about Italian food, most meals cooked with tomatoes and herbs are almost a sure hit. If there is an ingredient that one of your family dislikes, move on to another recipe or substitute a different spice, herb, or liquid. If you're a lazy cook, pick a simple recipe. Don't feel bad—it's just your style.

Cooking equipment deserves a few words. Of course, we all use what we have available, but there are times when pots and pans need to be replaced or when a hint about a cookware gift might be dropped. I find heavy-gauge metal pots and pans are better because the metal is thick, heating evenly with no hot spots. Therefore, they are more forgiving if the heat is too high and there is less chance of the food sticking to the pan. Cast-iron cookware fits the bill and is also inexpensive. But it is very heavy to lift and if it isn't coated, it needs to be *seasoned* each time you use it. The modern cast-iron pans are not the same as our grandmothers had. They were seasoned once and it held. However, my seasoning method takes only a minute or two. I wash the pan in hot, soapy water after each use, utilizing a plastic scraper if necessary. After rinsing, I put the pan on a hot burner until it is thoroughly dry. Then I dip a paper towel in a little cooking oil and rub it on the hot surface.

My very favorite pots and pans are made from heavy aluminum, sold under the brand name of *Calphalon*. They are stick resistant, scratch resistant, well made, lightweight, and also expensive. However, I expect them to last a lifetime or two.

A pair of tongs is a necessity in wild-game cookery. The meat has little natural fat and must not be pierced with a fork when turning and removing from a pan. I also use a big selection of wooden spoons and spatulas in different sizes for stirring and frying. They probably don't work any better than metal ones but it eliminates the grating noise of metal against metal and they don't harm the finish on pans. And somehow food seems to taste better when stirred with wooden utensils. Another must for gamebird cooking is a pair of poultry shears. They are very efficient and much safer to use than a knife when splitting a bird.

My favorite range top is gas powered. Electric ranges just don't respond quickly enough when the heat is turned up and down. However, I feel that an electric oven and broiler work better than gas.

Frost-free freezers are a menace to frozen game (and everything else). The fan pulls the moisture out of the packages and causes "freezer burn" within a short time. Just think about how fast unused ice cubes disappear and then you know what happens to game. The solution is a model without the frost-free feature. If that's not possible, double and triple wrapping will help protect the meat.

I serve gamebirds, waterfowl and many big-game dishes on individual wooden plates, especially if I'm going to use fillet or steak knives to carve or cut the meat. Wood won't dull the knives or cool the meat. The best wooden plates have grooves in the surface and a well on one end—like miniature platters. They are difficult to find but well worth searching for. I bought mine several years ago at a restaurant supply store that I found through my telephone yellow pages. If you can locate some, you'll love them— and they'll last a lifetime.

Some of my recipes call for whole and half gamebirds. Use these *only* for guests who are not afraid of tackling them with knife and fork—and finally fingers—to get those last tasty morsels. They are people who really appreciate wild game. When introducing gamebirds to company, choose a breast recipe where only the meat is served and the bones are left in the kitchen. They'll feel more comfortable and so will you.

Everything that is supposed to be served hot should be placed in or on warm dishes. There are many ways to heat them. If the oven isn't in use, set it at 150°F. and stick them in for about 10 minutes. Sometimes there is a burner on top of the range through which oven heat is vented: that's another place. The top of a toaster oven, radiator, a turned-on television or radio set are other options. It's worth the bother when your food arrives at the table piping hot.

Most of the ingredients I use in this book can be easily found in your local supermarket. With the exception of parsley, I usually use dried herbs. If fresh are substituted in the recipes, increase the amount a little. Dried herbs and spices lose their potency quickly and should be tossed out after a year or 18 months. It can be expensive to purchase new ones these days but if a few neighbors pool their money and buy in partnership, the cost can be cut considerably. Most of us don't use a whole jar of herbs or spices in a year. If you have trouble finding one of them in your supermarket, write to me in care of the publisher and I'll help find a mail-order source.

You'll find very few recipes where I specify the amount of salt. I've discovered over the last few years that when we gradually decrease the amount of salt we use, our taste changes and we don't demand as much—or in some cases, any. Many canned goods already have salt in them; bouillon cubes are salty and many natural foods such as celery and carrots contain salt. Try cutting down as I have and I think you'll agree that it's easy.

Occasionally you'll find a "pinch" of an herb or spice is called for. This is the amount you can hold between the *tip* of your thumb and forefinger. Use caution: more can always be added after tasting.

One of my short cuts in thickening sauces and gravies is Quick Mixing flour. You'll find it in the flour section of the market (Gold Medal label) in a shaker container. The flour is granulated and mixes in warm liquids without lumping, if it is stirred constantly. Regular flour, cornstarch, and arrowroot all have to be mixed with a cold liquid before adding to the hot. Flour does add a starchy flavor to gravies and sauces but most diners do not find it objectionable. Cornstarch and arrowroot produce a glossy sauce without altering the taste of the dish. It's your choice.

Buy the best quality wild rice you can find. It's all quite

expensive but most of us don't use enough during a year to scrimp on the price. And there's nothing else even close to its nutty flavor. The best place to buy wild rice is in Minnesota where it's grown. If you are there in person, you'll be able to buy top quality at bargain prices. Mail order is the next best choice. Check the food and outdoor magazines and catalogs and read the ads carefully. The rice should be relatively clean of foreign material and the grains long and plump. There is a big difference in the quality of wild rice: don't buy less than the best. For wild rice dishes and other recipes to serve with game, check the last chapter in this book, "Dishes to Accompany Game."

This next section on wine is by my husband Jim who is my in-house wine expert. I leaned on him too for the wine notes that accompany each species in the book.

I have long believed that wine writers write mostly for other wine writers. They might not start out that way, but sooner or later they realize that as their store of knowledge increases the pedestrian wine drinker and buyer probably won't understand what they're talking about. They don't intend to be snobbish— it's just that they can't help themselves. Those of us who try to decipher their code and do a spot of wine detective work on our own must muddle along as best we can. I am not a wine writer but I enjoy drinking the results of that happy chemical phenomenon called fermentation as a companion to good food—especially with wild game.

The old saw about red meat—red wine, white meat—white wine, or red with hooved meat and white with fish and fowl doesn't always apply with domestic meat and most decidedly doesn't with game. A cold, white wine with duck is totally out of place and would be, much of the time, with upland gamebirds unless they are prepared in a very plain manner. Some rabbit recipes would be served well with white wines and so might a few grouse or quail dishes, but on the whole, the reds will be generally more suitable with most gamebirds and mammals.

The basic reason for selecting red wines for game presentations is the life-style of wild creatures. They are not fed growth hormones or special diets nor are they pampered by agricultural husbandry. They live a fast, danger ridden and usually short existence. With few exceptions, the animals and birds we hunt and eat are under constant pressure from predators and the elements from the moment they leave the egg or nest. They move fast and in some cases long distances (the migratory birds) causing a muscle tone that is not present in domestic species. This does not always mean that wild meat will be tough (although it sometimes is), just different in texture and more intense in flavor. Since red wine usually has more "body" just like wild game, it has a more robust character. It's got more oomph! It's the right stuff with wild meat!

All of the foregoing ties in nicely with the mild revolution which is presently taking place in the wine growing regions of this country. Wine tastes are changing and we're drinking more wine with food. As this experience grows, wines that lean toward the dry, well-rounded types become more popular. The novice wine drinker almost always prefers a sweeter, less complicated style. In time, he discovers the delights of the more mature and subtle varieties.

The Cabernet Sauvignon grape as grown in France and California turns into beautiful wine for serving with many game recipes. The French version is usually a bit more acidic and the Californias somewhat softer. But these are broad generalizations— both countries make great Cabernet Sauvignon.

I'm very partial to Zinfandel wine from California. I think it's one of our best all-purpose wines for pouring with game. About the only things I wouldn't serve it with would be fish or shellfish. Just about every wine maker handles Zinfandel in a different way and the range is from very dry to spicy and aromatic. Jug Zinfandels are not expensive. Try a few labels until you find one that appeals to your palate.

The best Pinot Noirs in the world come from the Burgundy region of France and I like the ones from the Cotes du Rhone best. They are the finest wines of all with venison, pheasant, and most waterfowl. Some California makers are beginning to come up with some good examples of Pinot Noir and the future holds great promise. Some evening, with a meal of lightly broiled venison chops, try a bottle of vintage Pinot Noir and experience a double-barreled dose of pleasure!

Now it's time for you to tackle the recipes—remembering to use common sense and humor. Relax, and have fun cooking your wild game!

Gamebirds

My favorite way to prepare gamebirds is unconventional: I like to cook the breast meat fast and hot. Through trial and error I have decided that birds are best separated into pieces. Then the breast can be cooked a short time and will turn out tender and juicy. Most gamebird legs need lengthy cooking to become tenderized. This is especially true with wild birds. However, chicken and tame turkey also benefit from this treatment. If you cook a whole bird until the legs are done, the breast will be overcooked and probably dry. You'll be amazed the first time you cook a bird's breast fast and hot—the juice flows when you cut into it and the flavor is magnificent. Trust me and try it.

I've also included long cooking treatments for all of the game birds along with some hot, fast roasting recipes. If you are lucky enough to bag a young bird (or birds), you'll be able to enjoy the legs at the same meal, using a roasting method. If they are tough, simply save them for a leg recipe or one of the formulas in the "Odds & Ends" chapter. The breast meat on most gamebirds is ample for a meal; however, the legs are too tasty to waste.

If the gamebird is to be roasted whole, it should be plucked. The skin will protect the meat from drying. The other recipes can be prepared with skinned birds, unless otherwise noted in the recipe. (After a long day in the field, it is certainly easier to skin game.)

Birds can be dry plucked if they are warm. Start with the breast feathers, near the neck, pulling just a few at a time—being careful not to tear the skin. It helps to hold the skin with one hand while the other plucks. Some gamebirds, like grouse and quail, are harder to pluck than others because of their delicate skin; also older birds can be difficult because feathers are so deeply set.

Many people prefer to immerse the bird in boiling water before plucking. This loosens the feathers and also keeps them from floating all over the house. The size of the bird dictates the length of time it should be sloshed in the boiling water; a dove, quail, or woodcock requires 1 to 2 seconds, a pheasant, about 6 or 7. Avoid overdoing the boiling water treatment or the skin will be partially cooked. After the birds are plucked, remove the entrails. If the birds are to be skinned, the entrails can be removed in the field. Remove all of the lung (pink and spongy) material with the entrails. Save the heart, liver, and gizzard for recipes in the "Odds & Ends" chapter.

The cleaned birds may be covered with plastic wrap and stored in the refrigerator for up to two days. If the birds are to be frozen, double wrap well in plastic or aluminum wrap and an ample layer of freezer paper. Label as to species, age (if known), servings, and date. Large gamebirds can be frozen for 3 to 4 months; small ones should be cooked in a month or two. If possible, store in a freezer that does not contain the frost-free feature. To prolong storage life, small gamebirds can be frozen in a block of ice. This also provides maximum protection against freezer burn. Put enough birds for a meal in a washed, cardboard milk carton (or similar container) and cover with water. Freeze until solid, wrap in freezer paper and label.

PHEASANT

Discovering how old pheasants are is easier than with other gamebirds, but remember, a large pheasant isn't necessarily an old one. Pick a bird up by its lower beak; if it breaks or bends, it is probably a bird of the year and perfect for roasting whole. The spur on a young pheasant is softer and shorter than an older rooster.

One pheasant will serve two or three, depending on how hearty the appetites. To stretch a pheasant into four servings, offer extra dishes with the meal; appetizers, a soup course, and extra vegetables all help.

With most pheasant recipes, the best wine by far is a rich, aromatic Pinot Noir. This is the wine of Burgundy (France) and of other places recently. The California Pinot Noirs are different in character but the distinctive fullness of the grape is there. If this wine is too heady, another fine choice would be a Zinfandel. If you're really into buying American this is a perfect selection since this grape is grown to perfection only in this country.

Other good generic wines to try with pheasant are the Petite Sirah, Barbera and Merlot. Actually, wild pheasants have enough flavor to shine with a rich Cabernet (but I'd rather save that wine for a venison chop).

If the recipe calls for tomato sauce with highly pungent spices, an Italian Valpolicella or Chianti is not out of place.

Since the time my first book was published, my personal taste for wine has changed and I suspect that may also be the case with many Americans. I had previously suggested that some of the soft "Chablis type" wines, put up in jugs by the Californians, and the sweeter German Rieslings might be suitable for game-farm pheasants. They still are, if your taste buds are not yet attuned to the richer delights of the reds. However, the gamebird flavor is not totally bred out of pheasants raised in pens, and they are much better served with red as opposed to white.

For the transition from white to red, try a California or French Beaujolais. Generally these are young red wines that weren't designed for long keeping. They are usually robust enough but not yet too powerful for most roasted and broiled birds.

Recipe Notes:

Roast Pheasant—only a young pheasant that has been plucked—preparation time, about 5 minutes—pure, delicious pheasant flavor.

Pheasant With Wine—perfect for older birds—preparation time, about 20 minutes—meat will be tender and juicy, lightly wine flavored.

Pheasant In Tomato Bisque—good for older bird—preparation time, about 30 minutes—intense, creamy, tomato flavor.

Easy Pheasant Breast—any age bird—preparation time, about 20 minutes—delicately flavored, juicy meat.

Pheasant Madeira—any age bird—preparation time, about 30 minutes—slightly sweet and creamy.

Pheasant Stroganoff—the remains of a pheasant after breast was removed—preparation time, about 30 minutes—dish will appeal to those who like Italian food.

Pheasant Corn Chowder—any age bird legs—preparation time, about 35 minutes—New England–style chowder flavor.

Roast Pheasant

> 2 *young* pheasants, with skin
> ¼ cup melted butter
> ¼ teaspoon marjoram

Dry pheasants with paper towels and brush with melted butter. Sprinkle with marjoram. Place the birds on one side on a greased rack in a roasting pan. Place in a preheated 375°F. oven for 30 minutes. Remove the pan from the oven, turn the birds over and pour the rest of the butter over them. Roast another 30 minutes. If the skin isn't brown enough, place the birds under the broiler for a couple minutes (4 inches from the heat). Using poultry shears, cut the birds right down the middle. Serves 4. Serve on a wooden platter with little steak or fillet knives.

Note: "Juicy with super flavor."

• • • • •

Pheasant With Wine

  1 large pheasant, cut into four serving pieces
      Flour seasoned with salt & pepper
  2 tablespoons butter
  2 tablespoons cooking oil
  8 medium-size peeled carrots
  4 medium-size celery ribs
  4 peeled onions
12 whole mushrooms
  1 cup dry red wine
      Salt & pepper to taste

Using poultry shears, cut the legs off at the middle of the backbone and cut the breast into two sections. Place some flour on a piece of waxed paper and mix in some salt and pepper (just a shake or two). Roll the pheasant pieces in the flour. Heat the butter and cooking oil in a large, heavy skillet or a Dutch oven until it is sizzling hot. Using tongs, place the pheasant pieces in the skillet and brown, turning on all sides. Don't crowd the pieces. When the bird is nicely colored, remove the pieces from the pan and set aside for a few minutes.

Add a bit more cooking oil to the pan, if necessary, and brown the carrots, celery, onions, and mushrooms. Turn the vegetables until they are brown on all sides (over medium-high heat). Add wine to the pan and return the pheasant pieces to the skillet, making sure they are on the bottom and in the wine. Sprinkle everything with a little salt and pepper if you wish. Cover the pan tightly and turn the heat to low or simmer.

Cook until the meat on the lower leg is tender. If the pheasant is an old bird, this will take from $1\frac{1}{2}$ to 2 hours. About halfway through the cooking time, turn the pieces over with tongs. At the same time, add more wine if necessary. You'll want enough sauce left in the pan to ladle over the pheasant and vegetables when served.

Serve with hot bread and red wine. For hearty eaters, double the amount of pheasant in the recipe to serve 4.

Note: "A favorite."

•   •   •   •   •

Pheasant In Tomato Bisque

  1 or 2 pheasants, cut into serving pieces
    Flour
  2 tablespoons butter
  2 tablespoons cooking oil
  $\frac{1}{2}$ cup finely chopped celery
  $\frac{1}{2}$ cup finely chopped carrot
  $\frac{1}{4}$ cup finely chopped onion
  3 cups chopped fresh tomatoes (seeded) or canned
    ones
  1 cup beef bouillon
  2 tablespoons chopped parsley
  1 bay leaf
  4 whole cloves
10 peppercorns
  1 cup light cream (half & half or equal amounts of
    whipping cream and milk)
    Parsley sprigs

Roll the pheasant pieces in flour. Melt the butter and oil in a large heavy skillet over medium-high heat. Brown the pheasant pieces on all sides. Remove browned pieces from the skillet with tongs and set aside. Lightly fry the celery, carrots and onions in the pan for 5 minutes, turning often.

In a Dutch oven or heavy pot, heat the tomatoes and bouillon. Add the vegetables to the pot along with the parsley, scraping the skillet to remove all the brown bits. Put the bay leaf, cloves and peppercorns in a double piece of cheesecloth and tie tightly with string. Add bag to the pot along with the pheasant. Cover and simmer over low heat for about 1$\frac{1}{2}$ hours, until the pieces are tender. Remove the pheasant to a heated platter. Keep warm in a 150°F. oven.

Discard cheesecloth bag. Turn the heat under the pot to high and cook the tomato sauce down until it is thick. Add cream and heat to the boiling point over medium-high heat. Serve the creamy tomato sauce ladled over pheasant and hot cooked rice. Garnish with parsley. Place the rest of the sauce in a gravy boat for the table. 1 pheasant will serve 2 to 4 (depending on the appetites), 2 birds will serve 4 to 8.

Note: "Excellent."

• • • • •

Easy Pheasant Breast

> 1 pheasant breast
> 2 tablespoons butter
> ½ cup sliced mushrooms
> ¼ teaspoon marjoram
> Salt & pepper to taste
> ¼ cup dry vermouth (or dry white wine)

With a sharp fillet knife, remove the breast meat from the bone and slice into thin pieces. In a large frying pan, fry the mushrooms in the butter over medium-high heat. When the mushrooms are brown (about 5 minutes), add the pheasant slices and fry for about 5 minutes, turning often. Sprinkle with a little salt and pepper and the marjoram. Add the vermouth to the pan, turn the heat to high and stir until vermouth has evaporated. Serve immediately. Serves 2, double recipe for 4. If the recipe is doubled, increase the vermouth to ⅓ cup.

Delicious when served with "Spinach with Browned Butter" and "Garden Tomato Salad" (see "Dishes to Accompany Game" chapter).

Note: "Very, very good."

• • • • •

Pheasant Madeira

> 1 pheasant breast, cut into small bite-size pieces (about ½-inch square)
> 1 tablespoon butter
> 1 tablespoon cooking oil
> 2 tablespoons finely chopped onion
> 1 garlic clove, minced
> ¼ cup Madeira wine
> ¼ cup heavy (whipping) cream
> ¼ cup pine nuts (optional)
> Parsley sprigs

Melt butter and oil in a large skillet over medium-high heat. Fry onion and garlic for 7 minutes, until limp. Add pheasant pieces to pan and quickly brown them on all sides, turning often. Add Madeira to pan and toss pieces in it while evaporating the liquid over high heat. Add cream and pine nuts, toss the pheasant pieces in it and cook down. Add salt and pepper to taste and serve immediately. Don't overcook the pheasant or it will be tough. Garnish platter with parsley sprigs. Will serve 2. Double the recipe to serve 4, increasing the Madeira and cream to $\frac{1}{3}$ cup each.

Note: "Super."

• • • • •

Pheasant Stroganoff

1 pheasant, after breast has been removed
1 beef bouillon cube
1 tablespoon cooking oil
1 medium onion, chopped
1 clove garlic, minced
$\frac{1}{2}$ cup reduced pheasant broth
$\frac{1}{2}$ cup chopped mushrooms
1 can (10$\frac{3}{4}$-oz.) tomato soup, undiluted
1 cup sour cream
10 drops Tabasco sauce
Salt & pepper to taste
Cooked thin spaghetti
Parmesan cheese
Parsley sprigs

Cut the pheasant into pieces with poultry shears and place in a pot with enough water to cover. Add the bouillon cube, cover, and cook until the meat is tender. Remove the meat from the broth, cool, and strip from the bones. Cut into bite-size pieces. Reduce the broth by cooking over high heat until there is about $\frac{1}{2}$ cup left, strain to remove bones and save for the recipe. This can be done early in the day or even the day before.

In a skillet, fry the onion and garlic in cooking oil over moderate heat until tender, about 7 minutes. Add broth, mushrooms, tomato soup, sour cream, Tabasco, and pheasant meat. Stir well and check for salt & pepper. Cover and simmer for 30 minutes.

Serve ladled over hot, cooked spaghetti, garnishing with parsley. Sprinkle with cheese. Serves 4.

Note: "A Jim favorite."

• • • • •

Pheasant Corn Chowder

>   2 pheasant legs
>   1 teaspoon celery seed
>   1 chicken bouillon cube
>   1 teaspoon onion flakes
>   5 medium potatoes, cut into cubes
>   2 onions, chopped
>   1 rib celery with leaves, chopped
>   Corn cut from 4 ears (or 1 package frozen corn)
> $\frac{2}{3}$ cup chopped mushrooms
>   2 cups milk
>   Dash red pepper
>   4 tablespoons butter
>   Salt & pepper to taste
>   1 teaspoon chopped pimiento
>   Paprika
>   Chopped parsley

In a large pot, stew pheasant in 1 quart water with celery seed, bouillon, and onion flakes until the leg is tender. Cool and strip the meat carefully from the bones. Chop into small bite-size pieces. This can be done early in the day.

Use pheasant broth as base for chowder, adding enough water to make 1 quart of broth. Add potatoes, onions, and celery and cook in broth for 15 minutes. Add corn and cook another 5 minutes, until all the vegetables are done. Add chopped pheasant and mushrooms. Stir in milk slowly. Add red pepper, butter, pimiento. Taste and correct salt and pepper if necessary. Heat until very hot. Remove from stove and cool for 2 hours to marry flavors. Before serving, heat. Garnish with paprika and parsley. Serves 6 to 8.

Note: "Very good."

• • • • •

QUAIL

Most quail are so young and tender that their legs can be cooked at the same time as the breast meat and both will be tender and juicy. It's a delicate meat that needn't be overpowered with a heavy sauce.

Quail should be plucked for the roasting method which is my favorite recipe. However, the other treatments are also superb and can be prepared with skinless birds. (Plucking enough birds for several servings is a pain.)

With small quail, such as bobwhite, blue and Gambels, serve two for each adult diner. Mountain quail (a larger bird) will serve one. As with other birds, stretch your servings, if necessary, by adding hearty dishes to the meal.

There is no upland gamebird that can compare with the quail when the word *subtle* is used. The taste tells the palate immediately that this is a wild bird, but it says so with great restraint. And that's exactly the kind of wine that should be served with a roasted bird—rich in understatement. A fine California Chardonnay is about the best complement possible for showing off the best in quail done in a natural way. Chenin Blanc can be almost as good if it is not too fruity. On the other hand, if your tastes lean towards the sweeter wines, a Riesling is acceptable. Some of the jug Chablis types are also good quail companions, especially if the birds are "sauced up" with additional herbs.

A soft red wine is also fine with most quail recipes. A Beaujolais with the cream sauces would be nice and so would a medium Italian red such as a Valpolicella.

Recipe Notes:

Roast Quail—whole plucked birds—preparation time, about 5 minutes—pure, delicious quail flavor.

Burnt Pines Quail—plucked or skinned birds—preparation time, about 20 minutes—moist, slightly spiced, creamy flavor.

Virginia Quail—plucked or skinned birds—preparation time, about 35 minutes—rich, spicy, tomato taste.

Quail Charlie—skinned bird breasts—preparation time, about 30 minutes—light, delicately flavored, juicy meat.

Roast Quail

>8 quail (with skin)
>¼ cup melted butter
>¼ teaspoon marjoram
>Salt & pepper

Allow the quail to come to room temperature. Brush all over with melted butter and sprinkle each with a little marjoram, salt, and pepper. Place the birds upright in a large shallow oven dish or baking pan. Place in a preheated 450°F. oven. Roast for 25 minutes. Halfway through the cooking, pour the rest of the butter on the birds. Remove from the oven and place the quail, with tongs, on a heated platter. Allow them to sit for 5 minutes before serving. This will set the juices. Serves 4. If possible, serve on a wooden platter with small steak or fillet knives.

Note: "Super treatment for quail."

• • • • •

Burnt Pines Quail

>8 quail (may be skinless)
>Flour seasoned with salt & pepper
>¼ cup butter
>¼ teaspoon savory
>¾ cup chicken bouillon or stock
>¾ cup sour cream

Thoroughly dry quail with paper towels. Place ⅓ cup flour on a large piece of waxed paper and sprinkle with salt and pepper. Mix well and roll the quail in the flour mixture. Melt butter in a large, heavy skillet over medium-high heat. Brown quail on all sides in the hot butter. Sprinkle each bird with savory. Add the bouillon to the skillet, cover, and simmer for 25 minutes. Add sour cream to the pan, mix with the rest of the pan juices and roll the quail in the mixture. Cover and simmer for another 5 minutes. Serve the quail on a heated platter, spooning some of the sour cream/bouillon mixture over each bird. If the mixture seems a bit thick, add a little more bouillon before serving. Serves 4.

Note: "Delicious."

• • • • •

Virginia Quail

> 8 whole quail, may be skinned
> 1 large egg, beaten with 1 tablespoon water
> 1 cup fine, dry bread crumbs
> ¼ cup minced parsley
> Salt & pepper to taste
> 4 tablespoons butter
> 1 onion, sliced
> 16 ounces (1 pint) tomatoes
> ⅓ cup whipping cream
> 1 teaspoon oregano
> 1 tablespoon minced parsley

Beat egg and water in a small bowl. Mix the bread crumbs with ¼ cup parsley. Dip the quail in the egg mixture and then roll in the bread crumb mixture. Sprinkle each bird with a little salt and pepper.

Heat butter in a large frying pan and brown the birds on all sides. Remove them with tongs when they are brown. Add onion, tomatoes, cream, and oregano to the frying pan and bring to the boiling point, cutting the tomatoes into small pieces.

Place the quail back in the pan and spoon the sauce over them. Cover, reduce heat to simmer, and cook for 30 minutes, turning the birds once after 15 minutes. Serve with hot cooked noodles or rice, ladling the sauce over the birds and noodles or rice. Sprinkle the dish with 1 tablespoon of minced parsley. Serves 4.

Note: The quail will be moist and delicious. (I either make dried bread crumbs by putting bread slices in a 300°F. oven and then crushing them with a rolling pin when they are thoroughly dry or I buy them.)

• • • • •

Quail Charlie

Breast meat from 8 quail
$\frac{1}{4}$ cup flour mixed with salt & pepper
4 tablespoons butter
1 cup sliced mushrooms (preferably fresh)
$\frac{1}{3}$ cup dry vermouth
$\frac{1}{3}$ cup chicken stock
$\frac{1}{8}$ teaspoon garlic powder
$\frac{1}{2}$ teaspoon tarragon

Remove each side of the quails' breasts with a small, sharp fillet knife by running the blade between the meat and the breast bone. Remove skin too.

Melt the butter in a large frying pan and fry the mushroom slices over medium-high heat until crisp cooked, about 5 minutes. Remove mushrooms with a slotted spoon and set aside or push them up the sides of the frying pan.

Roll the breast pieces in flour that has been mixed with a little salt and pepper. Brown in the hot butter on both sides. Push the meat to one side and add the vermouth, stock, garlic, and tarragon to the middle of the frying pan. Mix well and stir meat and mushrooms into the liquid. Turn the heat to high and cook about 3 minutes, until the liquid has been reduced by one half. Serve immediately with the pan sauces ladled over the meat and mushrooms. Garnish with parsley sprigs. Serve with baked potatoes and a green vegetable. Serves 4.

Note: This is an elegant dish that can be served to guests who are not willing to pick up game birds to savor the last tender morsel. This way the delicious legs and backs are saved for another meal. See the "Odds & Ends" chapter for suggestions. Wrap the rest of the carcass well and freeze.

• • • • •

GROUSE

Grouse is the gamebird I grew up with and it's still a favorite to eat (although I have a hard time hitting them). The breast meat is so juicy and delicious when it's cooked hot and fast that I've included four recipes for this method. Only one recipe requires grouse with skin, but it's worth the extra effort of plucking them. In the rest of the recipes, the birds can be skinned before cooking.

To cut grouse into serving pieces, remove the legs at the hip joint with a thin-bladed knife. Then, using poultry shears, cut the breast into two pieces, severing the breast bone slightly off center.

Weighing in at a little over a pound, one grouse is an ample serving for one adult, or a small serving for two.

The taste of gamebirds varies just as wines do. To say that all dry wines taste alike, or that all sweet wines do, is just as much in error as would a similar statement be concerning upland birds. Grouse taste like grouse—nothing else. To the wine buff, an oaky Chardonnay might be the ideal selection and I wouldn't criticize that choice. However, there is something about the ruffed grouse that calls for more than a hint of fruitiness. Maybe it's because grouse are fond of wild apples, grapes, and assorted berries. When cooked in a natural way, grouse fairly sings with a German Moselle or a California Riesling from the northern counties. Even a rose wine made from Gamay grapes (if not too sweet) can be a fine companion.

If the grouse is "doctored" with extra herbs or flavorings, go with something that has more body, such as a Zinfandel or even a good Burgundy.

I've also mentioned Burgundy with other gamebirds. It's because the wines made from primarily Pinot Noir grapes blend so well with most wild game. The folks who write regularly of fermented grape juice are always talking about how Pinot Noir has that "earthy" quality. Well they're right. And game has that same magic ingredient. But on the other hand, it would be difficult to find a wine that would not somehow be enhanced by serving it with ruffed grouse!

Recipe Notes:

Turtle Creek Grouse—plucked birds—preparation time, about 10 minutes—lightly flavored, fruity taste.

Cherry Springs Grouse—skinned or plucked birds cut into serving pieces—preparation time, about 25 minutes—lightly spiced, creamy flavor.

Gooseberry Grouse—skinned or plucked birds—preparation time, about 20 minutes—tart, fruity, delicate flavor.

Grouse Nate—skinned bird, cut into serving pieces—preparation time, about 25 minutes—mildly pungent flavor.

Tasty Grouse Breast—skinned breasts—preparation time, about 15 minutes—mellow, creamy taste.

Broiled Grouse Breasts—skinned breasts—preparation time, about 15 minutes—rich, tangy flavor.

Turtle Creek Grouse

    2 grouse, with skin
    $\frac{1}{4}$ cup port wine
    $\frac{1}{4}$ cup butter
    $\frac{1}{4}$ cup orange juice
    2 tablespoons water
    $\frac{1}{2}$ teaspoon orange rind
    Parsley sprigs

Preheat oven to 450°F. and have grouse at room temperature. Heat port, butter, orange juice, water, and rind to the boiling point in a small saucepan. Place grouse upright in a roasting pan and pour a couple tablespoons of the hot port mixture over each. Put the pan in the oven and roast for 30 minutes, basting with the port mixture several times during the cooking.

Place the cooked birds on a heated platter. Scrape the bottom of the roasting pan to loosen any bits of meat and pour the sauce in a heated gravy boat. Serve with the birds, dolloping a little sauce on each slice of meat. Garnish with parsley.

2 large servings or 4 small ones. To serve 4, cut the birds in two with poultry shears.

Note: "Excellent—meat is very juicy and just beyond the pink stage."

•　•　•　•　•

Cherry Springs Grouse

> 3 grouse, cut into serving pieces
> Flour, seasoned with salt & pepper
> 3 tablespoons cooking oil
> 1 cup light cream (half & half or even parts of
>   whipping cream and milk)
> 1 cup dry red wine
> ⅔ cup sliced mushrooms
> ¼ teaspoon savory

Roll the grouse pieces in the flour mixture. Heat oil in a large skillet over medium-high heat. Brown the grouse on all sides in the hot oil. Using tongs, place the browned pieces in an oven-proof casserole. Add cream, wine, mushrooms, and savory to the frying pan. Heat and stir until the mixture is at the boiling point. Pour the mixture over the grouse, cover, and place in a preheated 350°F. oven for 1 hour. Serve the sauce in a heated gravy boat to be ladled over the grouse and hot, buttered rice (or noodles). Serves 4.

Note: "Great recipe."

• • • • •

Gooseberry Grouse

> 4 grouse
> Flour seasoned with salt & pepper
> 2 tablespoons butter
> 2 tablespoons cooking oil
> ⅓ cup cognac or brandy
> 1 can (1 lb.) gooseberries with liquid
> Pinch of tarragon
> 1 teaspoon sugar
> ⅓ cup orange juice
> Salt & pepper to taste

Roll grouse in the flour mixture. Heat butter and oil in a large, heavy skillet over medium-high heat. Brown the birds on all sides. Pour cognac, gooseberries, and orange juice over the browned birds and add the tarragon and sugar to the skillet. Dust the birds lightly with salt and pepper. Cover and simmer over low heat for 1 hour, turning the birds once during the cooking. Serve the grouse on a heated platter and the sauce in a gravy boat. 4 generous servings or 8 small ones.

Note: "Very good."

• • • • •

Grouse Nate

> 1 skinless grouse
> ½ cup white wine
> 2 tablespoons butter
> 1 green onion, chopped
> 2 tablespoons parsley, chopped
> ½ tablespoon Dijon-style mustard
> Salt & pepper
> Parsley sprigs

Cut the wings and legs from the grouse. Bone the breast into two fillets. Marinate the grouse pieces, in a nonmetal dish, for 4 hours in the white wine, turning frequently.

Fry the onion in a large skillet with the butter over medium-high heat. Add the grouse pieces, sprinkle with the parsley, a bit of salt and pepper, and fry for about 8 minutes, turning the grouse once. Remove the grouse pieces with tongs to a heated platter. Add the wine and mustard to the pan. Heat, scraping the pan until the wine is slightly reduced. Pour over the grouse and serve immediately. 2 small servings. Double the recipe if you wish.

Note: "Excellent."

• • • • •

Tasty Grouse Breast

> 2 grouse breasts
> 3 tablespoons butter
> 2 tablespoons Madeira wine
> ⅓ cup whipping cream
> Salt & pepper

Fillet the flesh from the grouse breasts into thin slices. Heat butter in a heavy skillet. When hot, add the grouse pieces and brown on all sides, turning often, over medium-high heat. Fry for about 3 minutes. Then add Madeira, turn heat to high, and cook liquid down, tossing the meat in the juice. Add cream and cook down until it is a little thick, tossing the grouse in the cream. Sprinkle with a little salt and pepper and serve immediately. Serves 4.

Note: "Absolutely perfect."

• • • • •

Broiled Grouse Breasts

> 2 grouse breasts
> ⅓ cup cooking oil
> 2 tablespoons soy sauce
> 1½ tablespoons brandy
> ¼ teaspoon celery salt
> Pepper

Break the breast bone on each grouse and press down firmly with the palm of your hand so they flatten out. Put the breasts in a flat, shallow dish. Mix the oil, soy sauce, brandy, celery salt, and a bit of pepper together and pour over the breasts. Turn them with tongs several times so they are covered with the marinade. Marinate for 1 hour, turning the meat a couple times.

Brush a basket grill with cooking oil and place the breasts in the basket, closing it so they are held tightly. Broil over a hardwood fire (in the fireplace or outside) for 4 to 5 minutes on each side, about 8 to 10 minutes total cooking time. The breasts will be tender and juicy and slightly pink close to the bone. To check doneness, cut into the thickest part of the meat with a sharp knife.

The breasts can also be broiled in the oven without the basket grill. Place them about 4 inches from a preheated broiler. Broil 8 minutes on the boney side, turn and broil 7 minutes. (Without the basket grill, the breasts tend to "pucker up" during the cooking and require a longer time because the meat isn't as flat.)

Serve with a green salad, hot bread, and wild rice. Serves 2 hearty appetites or 4 small ones.

Note: "Very good."

• • • • •

WOODCOCK & SNIPE

When you consider what a small bird the woodcock is, it's amazing how rich the meat is. As a member of the migratory group, its breast muscles work hard and that accounts for the intense flavor. I've heard a lot of people say they don't like woodcock—"it tastes like liver." My answer is, they have never had it cooked properly.

The woodcock is mostly breast meat so it is often skinned with only the breast being used. In this case, the legs, liver, heart and gizzard should be saved for recipes listed in the "Odds & Ends" chapter. I've included a recipe for roasting woodcock, but it's necessary to pluck them for that. The rest of the recipes can be followed with skinned birds. For an adult, serve two woodcock.

The best woodcock meals I've enjoyed have been washed down with Cabernet Sauvignon. The heady Bordeaux wines from the Medoc region or an equally aromatic Napa Valley red from California does the job to perfection.

No other gamebird has the heavy, earthy flavor of woodcock and it takes an equally potent wine to stand up to it. These woodcock recipes take advantage of this rich flavor and make no attempt to totally hide it. That wouldn't be fair to the woodcock. To serve a bland or sweet wine would be an injustice too.

Woodcock is the greatest meal I can think of to serve two or more bottles of Cabernet wine with (depending on the number of guests). Try one and then the other and let your guests play the part of wine experts and decide which one they like best. The woodcock will heighten the taste buds and make them more receptive to the subtle overtones of each bottle. It's good fun and if you have enough woodcock to entertain with, why not pull out the stops!

Recipe Notes:

Roast Woodcock—plucked birds—preparation time, about 5 minutes—pure woodcock flavor, juicy meat.

Broiled Woodcock—preferably plucked breasts (can be skinned)—preparation time, about 5 minutes—slightly sweet, very juicy meat (on the pink side).

Creole Woodcock—skinned woodcock breasts—preparation time, about 35 minutes—spicy, Louisiana-style dish.

Bangor Woodcock—skinned birds or breasts—preparation time, about 35 minutes—rich, creamy dish.

Roast Woodcock

> 8 plucked birds
> ¼ cup butter
> ½ cup Madeira wine

Melt the butter in a small saucepan, add the Madeira and heat to the boiling point. Put the birds in a shallow, flat, roasting pan and spoon a little of the hot butter/Madeira mixture over each. Place the pan in a preheated 450°F. oven. Roast the woodcock for 25 minutes, basting twice with the mixture. Serve the birds on a wooden platter. Put the rest of the butter/Madeira mixture in a heated sauce boat with the pan juices and serve ladled over the woodcock. Serves 4.

Note: "Excellent."

•　•　•　•　•

Broiled Woodcock

> 8 woodcock breasts, plucked or skinned
> ¼ cup butter
> ¼ cup orange marmalade

Dry the birds with paper towels and place on a greased broiler pan. In a small saucepan, heat the butter and marmalade. Spoon a little of the butter/marmalade mixture over each bird and place under a preheated broiler 4 inches from the heat. Broil for 8 minutes. Serve immediately. Will serve 4.

Note: "Delicious."

• • • • •

Creole Woodcock

> 8 woodcock breasts
> $\frac{1}{4}$ cup flour
> Salt & pepper
> 3 tablespoons cooking oil
> $\frac{1}{2}$ cup chopped onion
> $\frac{1}{2}$ cup chopped celery (including leaves)
> $\frac{1}{2}$ cup chopped green pepper
> $\frac{1}{2}$ cup uncooked long-grain rice
> 16 oz. (1 pt.) canned tomatoes plus water
> 1 bay leaf
> 1 tablespoon chopped parsley (or parsley flakes)
> 3 dashes Tabasco sauce

Mix flour with a dash of salt and pepper and roll the woodcock breasts in the mixture. Heat oil in a frying pan and brown the breasts on all sides. Place the rice in the bottom of an oven-proof casserole that has been buttered. Arrange the browned breasts on top of the rice in a single layer.

Add the onion, celery, green pepper, and parsley to the frying pan. Squeeze the juice out of the tomatoes into a measuring cup (don't press too hard) and add enough water to the tomato water to make 1¼ cups of liquid. Add the liquid and squeezed tomatoes to the frying pan with the Tabasco, bay leaf, and a dash of salt and pepper to taste. Bring to a boil, then pour the mixture over the woodcock. Cover the casserole with foil and place in a 350°F. preheated oven for 45 minutes. Discard the bay leaf and serve with hot bread and a green salad. Serves 4.

Note: "Great dish!"

• • • • •

Bangor Woodcock

    8 woodcock
       Flour
    4 tablespoons butter
    4 tablespoons cooking oil
    1 cup dry red wine
    1 teaspoon thyme
       Salt & pepper to taste
    1 onion, minced
    1 cup sour cream
       Shake of red pepper
    4 pieces of toast, cut diagonally in fourths

Cut the legs and breasts from the woodcocks. Roll the bird pieces in flour. Heat half the butter and oil in a large skillet over medium-high heat. Brown the pieces in the skillet on all sides. Add the wine, thyme, salt, and pepper to the skillet with the woodcock, cover and simmer for 1 hour or until the legs are tender.

In another skillet, fry the onion in the rest of the butter and cooking oil for 5 minutes over medium heat. Add sour cream and red pepper and mix well.

When the woodcock is tender, remove from broth. Cut the breast meat from the bone and place on toast points on heated plates. Add red wine mixture to the sour cream and cook down over high heat until the sauce is slightly thick. Ladle the sauce over woodcock breast meat on the toast. Place legs around the toast and serve garnished with parsley sprigs. Serves 4. (If only the breasts are cooked, reduce cooking time to 35 minutes.)

Note: "Super."

• • • • •

DOVE

Doves are migratory birds and the breast meat is rich, dark, and flavorful, like other long ranging birds such as woodcock, ducks, and geese.

Because 90% of the dove meat is in the breast, they are ordinarily the only part cooked in recipes. The little legs along with the liver, heart, and gizzard should be saved for recipes in the "Odds & Ends" chapter.

Doves are usually skinned because they are so small and it takes so many for a meal. However, there is no reason they cannot be plucked if time is available.

To freeze doves, put them in a washed, cardboard, milk container or a plastic freezer box. Fill the container with water, cover, and freeze solid. This will protect the little birds from freezer burn.

Three or four doves per person is a minimum adult serving. This can cause problems at the end of the season when you end up with just a few birds in the freezer. The doves can be combined with other game for recipes in the "Odds & Ends" chapter or they can be cooked for 45 minutes in your favorite spaghetti sauce and served over pasta. Prepared this way, two birds per serving is adequate.

As with most migratory birds, the breast meat of all doves is dark and flavorful, but for some reason, the taste doesn't hold up to extremely rich wines. Some of the California jug wines called "table reds" work well with doves. Many of them are blended in a way that, while honestly semidry, they still have a hint of sweetness. A young, French Beaujolais accomplishes the same thing in a slightly different way.

While I love the color of rose wine when served with doves, it's sometimes not easy to find a pink wine that isn't too sweet. I've had some bottles of Paul Masson Gamay Rose that filled the bill. The French Dame Rose is also a good label to look for if you like pink wines.

Recipe Notes:

Braised Doves—skinned birds or breasts—preparation time, about 10 minutes—delicately spiced flavor.

Hunter's Run Dove—plucked or skinned breasts—preparation time, about 15 minutes—pure dove taste.

Dove, Hungarian-Style—skinned birds or breasts—preparation time, about 35 minutes—rich, creamy dish.

Pickled Doves—skinned breasts—preparation time, about 20 minutes—pleasantly pungent flavor.

Braised Doves

12 to 16 doves
$\frac{1}{3}$ cup flour seasoned with salt & pepper
  (approximately)
2 tablespoons cooking oil
$\frac{1}{4}$ teaspoon savory
$\frac{1}{2}$ cup dry white wine

Roll the doves in the flour mixture. Heat the oil in a large skillet and brown the doves on all sides over medium-high heat. Sprinkle the doves with the savory. Pour the wine in the pan, cover it, and turn the heat to simmer. Cook for 45 minutes, adding a little water if necessary. Serves 4.

Note: "Simple but delicious."

•　•　•　•　•

Hunter's Run Dove

16 dove breasts
2 tablespoons cooking oil
$\frac{1}{2}$ cup Madeira wine
$\frac{1}{8}$ teaspoon savory
$\frac{1}{8}$ teaspoon freshly ground pepper
3 tablespoons butter
1 cup chopped mushrooms
  Parsley sprigs

Mix cooking oil, Madeira, savory, and pepper. Marinate the dove breasts in the mixture for 3 hours, turning them over several times. Place the breasts upright on a broiler pan and put under a preheated broiler 4 inches from the heat. Broil for 8 minutes, brushing with a little butter after 4 minutes.

While the breasts are broiling, fry the mushrooms in the butter for 5 minutes over medium-high heat. Add the marinade mixture and heat until reduced by half. Serve the breasts with a little of the mushroom mixture ladled over each breast. Serves 4. Garnish with parsley.

Note: "Super recipe—the meat will be slightly pink."

•　•　•　•　•

Dove, Hungarian-Style

16 doves, breasts or whole birds
Flour
Salt & pepper
$\frac{1}{4}$ cup butter or margarine
$\frac{1}{2}$ cup chopped onions
$\frac{1}{2}$ cup chopped celery
$\frac{1}{2}$ cup sliced carrots
1 cup chicken stock
1 cup sour cream
1 tablespoon Hungarian paprika
2 tablespoons chopped parsley

Roll doves in flour mixed with a little salt and pepper. Melt the butter in a large frying pan and brown the doves on all sides. Remove the doves from the pan. Add the onions, celery, and carrots and brown over medium-high heat for 5 minutes. Add the chicken stock, sour cream, paprika, and mix well. Put the doves back in the pan, ladle the sauce over them, cover the pan, and turn the heat to simmer. Cook for 40 minutes, adding more chicken stock if necessary. Sprinkle with parsley and serve with buttered noodles or boiled potatoes and a green salad. Serves 4.

Note: "Delicious."

• • • • •

Pickled Doves (Escabeche)

12 dove breasts
1 whole onion
2 carrots, sliced
2 garlic cloves
2 bay leaves
$\frac{1}{2}$ teaspoon marjoram
1 teaspoon peppercorns
$1\frac{1}{2}$ cups wine vinegar
$1\frac{1}{2}$ cups peanut oil
$\frac{1}{2}$ teaspoon salt

Place the dove breasts in a large saucepan with all the rest of the ingredients, being sure that the meat is covered with vinegar and oil. (Add more of each if it isn't.) Bring the mixture to a boil, reduce heat, cover, and simmer for about 45 minutes, until the breasts are tender. Place the doves in a sterilized glass jar (with a wide neck) and pour the vinegar/oil mixture over the meat until it is well covered. Place an air-tight lid on the jar and store in a cool but not cold place. The oil will congeal in the refrigerator— a cold cellar is perfect. Marinate for 24 hours before serving. Thoroughly dry doves on paper toweling and serve as an appetizer. The small breasts are excellent finger food for picnics or backyard parties. They can also be served on lettuce leaves as a first course. The doves can probably be kept several weeks in a cool place but it's difficult since they are so good.

Note: "Very good."

• • • • •

TURKEY

Ben Franklin believed that the crafty wild turkey should have been our national bird. Our biggest gamebird is a survivor because of its keen eyesight and acute hearing. On the other hand, the domestic turkey is rather dumb. There is also a remarkable difference in the taste of the two birds. The wild variety is packed with flavor; the tame turkey has relatively bland-tasting meat.

Most people are disappointed in the amount of breast meat on a wild turkey. There's no question about it, they are more streamlined. They work hard to live and it shows. Like other wild (and domestic) birds, if you roast a whole wild turkey to the point where the leg meat is tender, the breast will be on the dry side. Two of my recipes are for roasting, since that's what most people like to do with the big bird, but I've included a breast and leg treatment that I know you'll like. With roast birds, count on at least one pound per serving.

The food and wine writers of this land go into a tizzy each year at Thanksgiving time trying to come up with the right wine to serve with our national bird of autumn. Depending on what the gobbler is stuffed or cooked with, wines of all colors and persuasions have been tried and frankly, it doesn't seem to matter all that much. If the bird is cooked to a dry state, a sweet Riesling can be fine. If it's a moist, pungently stuffed model, a rich red Burgundy can also do the job. I once enjoyed a gloriously browned bird, filled with oysters and bread crumbs that tasted great with a California Chardonnay. And all of this goes for domestic and wild birds.

The wild birds are less fatty and as a result turn out drier than pen-reared birds. Since wild turkey is a very special meal and doesn't come along on a regular basis, why not go all the way and serve a dry or semidry champagne? Some of the French brut (extra dry) versions are a bit too austere for turkey but the "very drys" or "drys" are perfect. Throw caution and the budget out the window and try a bottle of Piper-Heidsieck, Taittinger, or Moet Chandon. You'll love it! If you can't find any of the French labels in your store, try California's Korbel, Kornell, or Schramsberg. If you like something a bit sweeter, but equally good with wild turkey, try the Great Western label from New York State.

If all of these wine selections sound strange to your palate, serve a cold pitcher of ale or beer with your wild bird and few will be disappointed—even those who don't usually drink beer. And the day after, a cold turkey sandwich with mayonnaise, a bit of mustard, and a lettuce leaf will be absolutely super with a cold bottle of beer. As a matter of fact, turkey is one of those meats that intensifies when cold. I don't know why this is so—it just is.

Recipe Notes:

Roast Turkey With Orange Dressing—whole plucked bird— preparation time, about 40 minutes—fruity flavor.

Roast Turkey With Oyster Dressing—whole plucked bird— preparation time, about 35 minutes—rich flavorful meat.

Fried Turkey Breast—skinless breast meat—preparation time, about 20 minutes—juicy, delicate meat with subtle herb flavor.

Hot Turkey Sandwich—rest of carcass after breast has been removed—preparation time, about 25 minutes—robust meal.

Roast Turkey With Orange Dressing

    1 wild turkey, plucked
      Soft butter
    $\frac{1}{2}$ cup orange juice
    $\frac{1}{2}$ cup butter
    1 teaspoon orange peel
      Orange Dressing (next page)

Dry turkey with paper towels. Stuff with Orange Dressing and close the body and neck cavities with skewers. With string, tie the wings close to the body and the legs together. Rub the turkey all over with soft butter. Place a double thickness of cheesecloth over the whole bird, put it on a rack in a roasting pan, and place in a preheated 350°F. oven. After 30 minutes, turn the heat to 325°F. Place the orange juice, ½ cup butter, and orange peel in a small saucepan and heat. Baste the turkey with this mixture every 20 to 25 minutes, coating the cheesecloth thoroughly. When the mixture is gone, use the pan juices to baste. Roast the turkey for 20 to 25 minutes per pound. Allow the turkey to rest on a heated platter while making the gravy. Remove the fat from the pan juices by skimming with a tablespoon. Pour the rest of the juices into a saucepan and thicken with flour mixed with water. Darken the gravy a little by adding a little Kitchen Bouquet. Add a little salt and pepper if necessary.

Orange Dressing:

¼ cup chopped onion
½ cup chopped celery
1 cup sliced mushrooms
¼ cup butter or margarine
1 orange, peeled, seeded, and diced
1 teaspoon grated orange peel
½ teaspoon poultry seasoning
1 chicken bouillon cube
6 cups dry bread cubes
Orange juice

In a large skillet, heat the butter and fry the onion, celery, and mushrooms for about 7 minutes, until they are tender. Add the diced orange, orange peel, poultry seasoning, and bouillon cube. Crush the cube and mix well. Add the bread and toss. Add enough orange juice to make a very moist stuffing (the moisture helps to keep the meat juicy). Heat well and stuff in the neck and body cavities of the turkey. Makes enough dressing for a 10-pound bird.

Note: "Excellent."

• • • • •

Roast Turkey With Oyster Dressing

  1 wild turkey, plucked
    Soft butter
  $\frac{1}{2}$ cup dry vermouth or white wine
  $\frac{1}{2}$ cup butter
  $\frac{1}{2}$ teaspoon thyme
    Oyster Dressing (below)

Dry turkey with paper towels and stuff with Oyster Dressing. Close the neck and body cavities with skewers. Tie the wings close to the body and the legs together with string. Rub the turkey well with soft butter and place on a rack in a roasting pan. Cover the bird completely with a double thickness of cheesecloth. Place the vermouth, $\frac{1}{2}$ cup butter, and thyme in a small saucepan and heat. Put the turkey in a preheated 350°F. oven and roast for 30 minutes before turning the heat to 325°F. Baste every 20 minutes with the vermouth mixture until it is gone. Then use the pan juices. Roast for 20 to 25 minutes per pound. Let the cooked turkey rest for 15 minutes on a preheated platter. Make gravy with the pan juices. Remove the fat and thicken with flour, adding a little Kitchen Bouquet to darken the gravy if necessary. Add a little salt and pepper if you wish.

Oyster Dressing:

  $\frac{3}{4}$ cup chopped celery
  $\frac{1}{2}$ cup chopped onion
  $\frac{1}{4}$ cup butter or margarine
  2 tablespoons chopped parsley
  1 crumbled bay leaf
  1 teaspoon poultry seasoning
  2 dozen oysters, chopped
  6 cups dry bread cubes
  2 eggs, beaten
    Oyster liquid and milk (half & half)
    Salt & pepper

In a large skillet, heat the butter and fry the celery and onion for about 7 minutes. Add the bay leaf, poultry seasoning, oysters, and bread crumbs. Toss this mixture and add the beaten eggs and mix well. Moisten with enough oyster liquid and milk to make a very moist dressing (to help moisturize the bird). Salt and pepper to taste; heat and stuff the turkey's neck and body cavities. Makes enough for a 10-pound bird.

Note: "Great."

•　•　•　•　•

Fried Turkey Breast

> 1 turkey breast
> ½ cup cooking oil
> ½ cup dry vermouth
> 1 teaspoon celery salt
> 1 teaspoon chervil (or parsley flakes)
> ½ teaspoon savory
> Salt & pepper
> Parsley sprigs

With a sharp fillet knife, separate the meat from the breast bone, scraping the bone to get all the meat. Cut the meat, against the grain, into thin (about ¼-inch) slices. If possible, remove the white tendon that runs down the middle of the breast before slicing. If it doesn't pull out easily, you can remove it as you slice. Put the slices in a nonmetal bowl with the cooking oil, vermouth, celery salt, and chervil. Mix well and marinate for about 3 hours. Heat a large frying pan and add 3 tablespoons of the marinade. Over high heat, fry the turkey slices quickly for about 2 minutes on each side, turning with a spatula. Don't overcook or the meat will be tough. Add more marinade if necessary. Place the cooked meat on a heated platter in a preheated 150°F. oven until all are done. Serve immediately, garnishing with parsley sprigs. Two pounds of breast meat will serve 4.

Note: "Very good."

•　•　•　•　•

Hot Turkey Sandwich

> 1 wild turkey carcass, legs and wings
> $\frac{1}{4}$ cup finely chopped onion
> $\frac{1}{4}$ cup finely chopped celery with leaves
> 1 beef bouillon cube
> 1 bay leaf
>   Flour
>   Kitchen Bouquet

Remove the turkey skin and cut the legs and wings off the carcass. Cut the carcass into manageable pieces with game scissors. Put them all in a large pot with the onion, celery, bouillon cube, bay leaf, and enough water to cover all. Cover, bring to a boil, turn heat to simmer, and cook until the leg meat is fork-tender. Remove the meat and allow it to cool. Then pull it off the bones in large chunks. Remove the bay leaf from the broth. Thicken the broth by putting flour in a large jar with some cool broth and shaking well. The amount of flour depends on how much broth there is. Try $\frac{1}{3}$ cup at first. Pour the flour mixture into the broth, heating and stirring until it thickens. Add a little Kitchen Bouquet to darken the gravy. (The dish can be held at this point for an hour or so.) Heat the gravy until it's bubbling hot and add meat. Count on at least one cup of meat per sandwich (more if you like a fat sandwich). While the meat is heating, place a slice of bread on each serving plate which has been preheated. With a slotted spoon, place meat on the bread. Top with another slice of bread and ladle gravy generously over the bread. Serve immediately.

Note: "Delicious."

• • • • •

CHUKAR

Chukar partridges are flavorful little birds but, for some reason, they tend to be a little tougher than many other gamebirds. Perhaps their quick bursts of speed take extra energy. I have found very few chukars that can be satisfactorily roasted and prefer the longer, moist, cooking methods. Two of the recipes in the "Pheasant" section work well with chukars—"Pheasant With Wine" and "Pheasant In Tomato Bisque." Or, use one from this section that has been specially designed for the little gamebird. Serve one chukar per person.

Wild chukars are tough little birds but they have superb flavor—not gamey but intense. If you know your birds were born in the wild, a heady Pinot Noir is a fine "show-off" wine. If they came from game-farm stock, a California jug Burgundy will be satisfactory, but a better choice will be a Barbera or Petite Sirah. There are just some wines that go with some meats perfectly and Petite Sirah and chukars is such a combination. The two best wines of this varietal grape I've tasted are Caymus Vineyards and Geyser Peak. They won't be cheap but they're worth the looking and the price. Petite Sirah wine is very deep purple, almost black in its best forms, and fills the mouth with heavy spice and a kind of earthy warmth.

Recipe Notes:

Tomatoey Chukar—birds cut in half—preparation time, about 20 minutes—rich, spicy dish.

Braised Chukar—birds cut into serving pieces (can be skinned)—preparation time, about 25 minutes—robust dish.

Savory Chukar—skinned chukar breast meat—preparation time, about 25 minutes—creamy flavor.

Chukar With Port—birds cut in half (can be skinned)—preparation time, about 20 minutes—pungent, spicy flavor.

Tomatoey Chukar

> 4 chukars, cut in half
> 2 tablespoons butter or margarine
> 2 tablespoons cooking oil
> $\frac{1}{2}$ cup chopped onions
> 1 10$\frac{3}{4}$-ounce can tomato soup
> 1 cup beer
> $\frac{1}{2}$ teaspoon curry powder
> $\frac{1}{2}$ teaspoon savory
> Parmesan cheese

In a large skillet, brown the skin side of the birds in hot butter and cooking oil over medium-high heat. As they are browned, transfer them to a roasting pan, skin side down in a single layer. Cook the onion in the skillet for about five minutes. Add the soup, beer, curry powder, and savory. Mix well and heat to the boiling point, turn the heat down, and simmer for five minutes. Pour the sauce over the chukars. Cover the pan and place in a preheated 375°F. oven. Bake for 1½ hours, turning the chukars over after 45 minutes. Serve on a bed of hot buttered noodles and ladle the pan sauce over all. Sprinkle amply with Parmesan cheese and garnish with parsley sprigs. Serves 4.

Note: "Great."

• • • • •

Braised Chukar

      4 chukars, cut into serving pieces
      ⅓ cup flour
        Salt & pepper
      3 tablespoons cooking oil
      1 large onion, sliced
      ½ teaspoon savory
      1½ cups water
      1 chicken bouillon cube
      ¼ cup milk
      2 tablespoons flour

Place the flour with a little salt and pepper in a paper bag. Add the pieces of chukar, a few at a time, and shake well to coat with flour. Add more flour to the bag if necessary. Heat the cooking oil in a Dutch oven and brown the meat on all sides over medium-high heat. Remove the pieces as they are browned with tongs and save until all are done. Add the onions to the pot, return the meat, and sprinkle the savory over the pieces. Add the water and bouillon cube, cover, and simmer until the birds are tender, about $1\frac{1}{2}$ hours. Remove the bird pieces to a heated platter. Mix the flour with the milk and add to the pan juices, stirring and heating until the gravy is thick. Serve with the meat and boiled potatoes. Serves 4 to 6.

Note: "Very good."

•   •   •   •   •

Savory Chukar

       Breast meat from 4 chukars
2 tablespoons butter
2 tablespoons cooking oil
$\frac{1}{3}$ cup finely chopped green onion
$\frac{1}{8}$ teaspoon savory
       Salt & pepper
3 tablespoons Madeira wine
$\frac{3}{4}$ cup heavy (whipping) cream
       Shake of red pepper
3 tablespoons minced parsley

    In a large, heavy skillet, fry the green onion in the butter for 5 minutes. Remove the meat from the birds and cut into small bite-size pieces. Add the pieces to the skillet, sprinkle with savory and a little salt and pepper, and brown on all sides quickly. (Don't overcook or the meat will get tough.) Add the Madeira and toss the meat in it. Add the cream and red pepper and heat thoroughly until bubbling hot. Serve on hot buttered rice and sprinkle with parsley. Serves 4. Save the rest of the birds for recipes in the "Odds & Ends" chapter.

Note: "Excellent."

•   •   •   •   •

Chukar With Port

     4 chukars, cut in half
     3 cups port wine
     5 whole cloves
     1 small onion, sliced
     1 bay leaf
     ½ teaspoon thyme
       Flour
       Salt & pepper
     3 tablespoons cooking oil

Place the wine, cloves, onion, bay leaf, and thyme in a sauce-pan and bring to a boil; turn the heat down and simmer for 5 minutes. Remove from the heat and allow the marinade to cool to room temperature. Put the chukars in a nonmetal container and pour the cool marinade over them. Cover and refrigerate for 24 hours, turning the chukars occasionally during the period. Dry the birds on paper towels and reserve the marinade. Mix some salt and pepper with some flour and roll the chukars in it. Brown the birds in hot oil until golden and place in a baking dish. When all are brown, add the reserved marinade to the pan and heat. Scrape the pan to deglaze and pour the liquid over the birds. Cover and put in a preheated 325°F. oven for 1½ hours, until tender. Turn the birds over halfway through the baking time. Serves 4.

Note: "Very good."

• • • • •

Waterfowl

The meat on ducks and geese is dark, rich, and full flavored. One of the biggest problems when discussing waterfowl is persuading cooks to try it on the medium-rare side. If you have never fixed it this way, you have a treat coming—the breast meat is pink, juicy, and succulent. The only drawback is that the legs on an older bird can be a bit tough. Unfortunately, it's difficult to tell the age of waterfowl. Youngsters can be large birds, small ones can be old-timers; it depends on the parents' genes. The breast meat will be tender when cooked with all my recipes. Luckily, there is enough breast meat for ample servings. So if the legs are on the tough side, they can be saved for another recipe.

With most of my recipes, it's best to have plucked birds; the skin protects the flesh from drying out in the cooking process. Dry plucking is fairly easy if the bird is still warm. Start on the breast at the neck and pull, between thumb and forefinger, a few feathers at a time. Hold the skin with the other hand to avoid tearing it. The problem with dry plucking is that the down flies *everywhere*. However, it can be saved to stuff pillows, clothing, etc.

Wet plucking is more popular with some hunters. Bring a pail of water to a boil, then slosh the bird up and down for a few seconds to soak and loosen the feathers. Small ducks take about six seconds; large ones, about 10 seconds; and geese, around 15 seconds. Don't leave the bird in the water *too long* or the skin will be partially cooked.

Save the heart and liver for recipes in this section or in the "Odds & Ends" chapter. When removing entrails, be sure to discard all of the lung material (pink and spongy). Singeing over a gas flame will remove residual hair and pinfeathers. Wash under cold water, both inside and out. Wipe the duck or goose with paper towels and store in the refrigerator up to two days or in the freezer for up to six months. Before freezing, double wrap in high quality plastic wrap and freezer paper and label with species and date.

To remove a whole duck or goose breast (for "Shadow's Broiled Duck Breast" or "Pymatuning Goose Breast"), use a heavy butcher's knife and begin at the rear of the breast. Run the knife blade along the natural separation above the rib cage towards the neck. When you reach the wings, search for the joint next to the breast. Cut through the tendons and remove the whole breast (with bone). It may be a little tough to do the first time, but the results are worth the trouble.

DUCK

Wild duck cooked to the medium-rare stage is one of my favorite meals. The flavor is rich, yet distinguished. If possible, serve whole or half ducks on wooden platters (described in the introduction to this book). Duck skin is tough and should be tackled with a sharp fillet or steak knife; wooden platters are preferable because china or pottery will dull knives in short order.

To cut hot ducks in half before serving, put a clean rubber glove on one hand (to protect it from the heat) and use poultry shears to sever the duck down the middle of the backbone and just to one side of the breast bone. Serve ducks as quickly as possible since the meat of dark-fleshed birds cools quicker than light-fleshed ones.

One large duck (mallard, black, pintail) will serve two; one small one (wood duck, teal) will serve one. For *hearty* appetites, serve one large duck per person.

Duck meat shines with a good Cabernet Sauvignon. If you want to show off and price is no object, serve your ducks with a Chateau Lafite, Margaux, Latour, or Rothschild—but be prepared to pay a bundle for any bottle over five years old. Anything much younger will be too harsh. For a little less money, look for a Robert Mondavi Reserve, Charles Krug, Beaulieu, or any one of the good "boutique" labels your wine merchant recommends. For a lot less money (less than $4), try to find a bottle of Romanian Premiat Cabernet Sauvignon—it's excellent.

Recipe Notes:

Apple Roast Duck—whole plucked birds—preparation time, about 35 minutes—delicate flavor, brings out the best in ducks.

Echo Lake Duck—plucked whole birds—preparation time, about 25 minutes—sweet, fruity flavor.

Braised Duck—skinned birds, cut in two—preparation time, about 20 minutes—hearty, rich dish for those who enjoy the well-done treatment.

Shadow's Broiled Duck Breast—plucked breast—preparation time, about 10 minutes—lovely, pungent taste.

M & M Roast Duck—plucked whole birds—preparation time, about 10 minutes—delicate, fruity taste; pink meat.

Broiled Duck—plucked birds, cut in half—preparation time, about 5 minutes—spicy flavor.

Duck Salad—skinned legs, wings, and backbones—preparation time, about 40 minutes—rich luncheon or first course dish.

Apple Roast Duck

        2 large ducks or 4 small ones
          Stuffing (below)
        1 small onion, chopped
        1 small carrot, chopped
        1 rib celery, chopped
        1 cup apple juice
        2 tablespoons brandy
        2 tablespoons butter

Stuff ducks with warm stuffing. Butter a flat, oven-proof casserole that is large enough so the ducks are not touching each other. Sprinkle the onion, carrot, and celery over the bottom and place the ducks on top of the vegetables. Heat the apple juice, brandy, and butter in a small pan and pour half of the mixture over the ducks. Place the ducks in a preheated 400°F. oven. Total cooking time will be 45 minutes for large ducks (35 to 40 minutes for small ones). After 15 minutes, pour half of the remaining apple mixture over the ducks quickly so little oven heat is lost. After another 15 minutes, pour the rest over the birds. 10 minutes before they are done cooking, turn the oven heat to 450°F. to brown the duck skin. Ducks will be tender and juicy and slightly pink near the bone. Cut the ducks in two or carve and serve at the table. Will serve 4.

Stuffing:

> 1 tablespoon butter
> 1 small onion, chopped
> $\frac{1}{2}$ teaspoon thyme
> 1 beef bouillon cube
> 5 slices bread, cut into $\frac{1}{2}$-inch cubes
> $\frac{1}{2}$ cup hot water

Cook onion in butter in a small frying pan. Add thyme, bouillon cube, bread, and water. Crush bouillon cube, mix well. Stuff ducks.

Note: "Great recipe."

• • • • •

Echo Lake Duck

> 2 large ducks or 4 small ones
> $\frac{1}{2}$ cup wild rice
> $\frac{1}{2}$ cup sliced mushrooms
> 3 tablespoons butter
> Soft butter
> Marmalade sauce (below)
> Parsley or watercress sprigs

Wash wild rice and cook in plenty of salted boiling water until tender, about 35 minutes. Rinse well under hot water and drain thoroughly. Fry the mushrooms in butter for 5 minutes. Add rice and toss. Have ducks at room temperature and stuff them with the hot rice mixture. Rub the skin with soft butter. Place the ducks in a buttered roasting pan and put in a preheated 425°F. oven. After 5 minutes, baste with hot marmalade sauce. Total roasting time is 40 minutes (30 minutes for small ducks). Baste every 10 minutes with sauce. Place cooked ducks on a heated platter and garnish with parsley or watercress. Add the rest of the sauce to pan juices, heat, and scrape the pan. Serve in a heated gravy boat to be ladled over duck slices. With poultry shears, cut the ducks in half. Serve immediately. Serves 4. Meat will be on the pink side.

Marmalade Sauce:

> $\frac{1}{3}$ cup lime marmalade
> $\frac{1}{3}$ cup orange juice
> 2 tablespoons butter
> $\frac{1}{2}$ teaspoon orange rind
> $\frac{1}{4}$ cup Madeira wine

Mix everything in a small saucepan and heat to the boiling point. Baste ducks.

Note: "Super recipe."

• • • • •

Braised Duck

> 2 large ducks or 4 small ones, skinned or plucked
> 1 onion, chopped
> 2 ribs celery, chopped
> $\frac{1}{4}$ cup port wine
> 1 cup water
> 1 tablespoon steak sauce
> $\frac{1}{2}$ teaspoon curry powder
> Salt & pepper

Cut the ducks in half with poultry shears. Oil a large roasting pan and sprinkle the onion and celery on the bottom. Place the ducks, breast side down, on the onion/celery mixture. Mix the port, water, steak sauce, and curry powder with a little salt and pepper and pour over the ducks. Cover and place in a preheated 450°F. oven for 20 minutes. Turn heat down and cook for another 1½ hours at 350°F. Check the water level once or twice and add more if necessary. Serve the ducks with the pan juices ladled over them. Will serve 4.

Note: "Good."

• • • • •

Shadow's Broiled Duck Breast

> 2 large plucked breasts or 4 small ones
> Soft butter
> 1½ tablespoons Dijon-style mustard
> ¼ cup Madeira wine
> ¼ cup butter
> ¼ teaspoon marjoram
> 1 tablespoon tomato paste
> ⅓ cup hot water

Place the duck breasts on a broiler pan that has been covered with heavy duty aluminum foil with the edges turned up. Rub the breast skin with soft butter and place in a preheated broiler, about 4 inches from the heat. In a small saucepan, mix the mustard, Madeira, butter, marjoram, tomato paste, and water and heat to the boiling point.

After the breasts have been broiling 10 minutes (5 minutes for small ducks), baste them with the sauce. Continue basting for the rest of the cooking time, about 10 minutes. Remove meat to a heated platter and pour the liquid from the sheet of aluminum foil back into the saucepan. Heat and pour in a heated sauce boat to be served ladled over *thin* slices of breast meat. Meat will be pink. Serves 4.

Note: "Delicious."

• • • • •

M & M Roast Duck

> 2 large ducks or 4 small ones
> Soft butter
> ¼ cup butter
> ½ cup dry red wine
> ¼ cup orange juice
> ¼ teaspoon savory
> Parsley sprigs

Dry the ducks with paper towels and rub with soft butter. Place in a roasting pan and put in a preheated 450°F. oven. Roast for 10 minutes. Heat the ¼ cup butter, red wine, orange juice, and savory in a small saucepan. After 10 minutes, turn the oven heat down to 350°F. and baste the ducks with ⅓ of the mixture from the saucepan. Roast for an additional 45 minutes (35 minutes for small ducks), basting two more times with the mixture. Remove the ducks from the oven. Cut the large ducks in equal halves and serve each on a wooden platter with a little of the roasting pan juices spooned over each one. Garnish with parsley. Serves 4.

Note: "Delicious."

• • • • •

Broiled Duck

> 2 large ducks with skin
> 1 bottle Italian salad dressing

Cut the ducks lengthwise with game scissors. Make the cut just to one side of the breast bone to separate the breast meat evenly. Place the duck halves in a large, flat, glass dish, such as a lasagna pan. Pour the bottle of salad dressing over the ducks, turning the birds several times to coat them well. Marinate for 3 hours, turning occasionally.

Place the ducks, skin side down on a broiler pan. Put in a preheated broiler 4 inches from the heat. Broil for 5 minutes. Turn the ducks over with tongs. Broil for 7 minutes. Serve immediately on wooden platters with sharp knives.

If the ducks are old, the legs may be a bit tough. They can

be saved for a recipe from the "Odds & Ends" chapter. Serves 4 normal appetites or 2 hearty ones.

Note: "Breast meat is delicately pink and succulent."

• • • • •

Duck Salad

>2 large duck backbones, legs, and wings
>1 beef bouillon cube
>½ cup plain yogurt
>¼ cup reduced duck broth
>3 drops Tabasco
>2 tablespoons catsup
>1 teaspoon steak sauce
>Salt & pepper to taste
>Paprika
>Lettuce leaves
>One or more of the following: tomato wedges, hardboiled egg wedges, chunks of celery, mushrooms, avocado slices, cucumber slices, radishes, ripe olives, or minced green onion.

Place the duck in water to cover with the bouillon cube and simmer until all the meat is tender. Remove from the broth, strip the meat from the bones, cover, and refrigerate.

Strain the broth to remove bones; cool in refrigerator until the fat congeals on top. Remove the fat and cook the broth down to ¼ cup. Chill again.

Mix sauce of yogurt, broth, Tabasco, catsup, and steak sauce and chill overnight. Arrange lettuce leaves on salad plates. Arrange the pieces of duck meat on the lettuce along with the tomato wedges or whatever you wish to use from the list above. Spoon the sauce over the salad and sprinkle with paprika. Serve with hot rolls. Serves 4.

Note: "Good."

• • • • •

GOOSE

Goose meat is rich, hearty, and succulent—especially when it's cooked to the pink stage. While I've included a long-cooking recipe, my favorite ones are hot and fast when the meat turns out on the rare side. The meat dries out in many goose recipes but my preferred ones will be juicy as well as tender. Try them and you'll be a convert.

A large goose breast will easily serve four. If the legs are on the tough side, reserve them (and the wings and backbone) for one of the last two recipes in this chapter, or the cooking methods in the "Odds & Ends" chapter.

Save the goose liver and heart; they are big and delicious (I've included a recipe for each). If you are hunting at a commercial goose-shooting area and hire someone to pluck and clean your geese, ask them to keep the organs for you. However, check the livers to be certain that the gall bladder has been removed or they will spoil within a few hours.

Tip: Use a thin carving knife to cut the cooked goose breast meat into paper-thin slices (like London broil). Sliced this way an older bird will be just as tender as a young one. Don't tarry on the way to the table: goose, like most dark meats, cools quickly.

Goose has more flavor per cubic inch of meat than any game-bird or mammal I've ever tasted. It will stand up to any wine and overpower all but the most assertive. To drink a bland or sweet wine with goose would be like drinking a glass of cider with a dill pickle. You could do it, but the combination of tastes would be much less than pleasant.

I'd go with the best Pinot Noir I could find with the goose—a hearty French Cotes du Rhone or, if you're up to it, an eye-crossing Spanish Rioja that still has a bit of the earth in it. If you're in doubt about all of this and want to play it safe, a California Zinfandel will do it here too.

Recipe Notes:

Roast Goose—whole plucked bird—preparation time, about 10 minutes—pure and rich flavor.

Wild Goose Apricot—whole skinned or plucked bird—preparation time, about 15 minutes—sauce is fruity; meat not unlike roast beef; great recipe for those who like their goose well done.

Pymatuning Goose Breast—plucked breast—preparation time, about 15 minutes—pungent taste.

Middle Creek Goose Breast—skinned breast—preparation time, about 25 minutes (includes preparation of "Hunt Sauce")—robust dish.

Goose Liver Pâté—preparation time, about 20 minutes—richly flavored appetizer.

Pickled Goose Hearts—preparation time, about 20 minutes—lightly spiced.

Delaware Valley Goose—cooked goose meat—preparation time, about 25 minutes—rich and filling.

Creamy Goose Sauce—cooked goose meat—preparation time, about 35 minutes—hearty dish.

Roast Goose

    1 5- to 6-pound goose
    1 onion sliced
    1 peeled and cored apple, sliced
    $\frac{1}{4}$ cup butter
    $\frac{1}{2}$ cup dry red wine

Have the goose at room temperature. Place it in a roasting pan and rub the skin with soft butter. Pour half of the wine ($\frac{1}{4}$ cup) in the roasting pan. Put the rest of the wine and the butter in a small saucepan and heat. Place the goose in a preheated 500°F. oven and baste every 5 minutes with a little of the wine and butter mixture. Roast for 35 to 40 minutes. Serve the pan juices in a heated serving bowl to be ladled over *very thin* slices of goose. Will serve 4 to 6. Meat will be medium rare.

Note: "Great."

•   •   •   •   •

Wild Goose Apricot

> 5- to 6-pound goose, may be skinned
> $\frac{1}{4}$ cup flour
> 1 10$\frac{1}{2}$-oz. can beef broth or consommé
> 1 teaspoon Kitchen Bouquet
> 1 1-pound can apricots, cut into chunks
> $\frac{1}{2}$ cup apricot syrup

Place the flour, beef broth, Kitchen Bouquet, apricots, and $\frac{1}{2}$ cup of the syrup from the apricots in a large, oven cooking bag. Shake gently to mix them well. Add the goose and turn several times to coat well with the sauce. Put a couple of the apricot chunks in the cavity. Close the bag according to manufacturer's directions and place in a roasting pan. Put the goose in a preheated 350°F. oven and cook for 2 to 2$\frac{1}{2}$ hours, until the legs wiggle easily. Place the goose on a heated platter and serve with the pan juices. They may be thickened but are very good as is. Serve them in a heated gravy boat, to be ladled generously over the goose. Serves 4 to 6.

Note: "Very good."

• • • • •

Pymatuning Goose Breast

> 1 plucked goose breast with the breast bone
> $\frac{1}{4}$ cup butter
> $\frac{1}{4}$ cup port wine
> 1 tablespoon steak sauce
> 1 tablespoon tomato paste
> 1 tablespoon prepared mustard
> $\frac{1}{2}$ cup water
> $\frac{1}{4}$ teaspoon savory

Rub the goose skin with soft butter and place it breast side down on a piece of aluminum foil that has been turned up on the sides. Place the foil on a broiler pan and place in a preheated broiler, about 4 inches from the heat. Broil 10 minutes.

While the goose is broiling, mix the butter, port, steak sauce, tomato paste, mustard, water, and savory in a small saucepan and heat to the boiling point.

After 10 minutes, turn the goose breast over on the foil and broil for another 18 minutes on the top side. After 5 minutes, start basting regularly with the sauce, using a little more than half of the sauce. Place the broiled breast on a heated platter. Pour the juices from the foil back into the saucepan, heat and serve in a heated gravy boat. Cut the breast meat into *very thin* slices and ladle a little sauce over each. Serves 4.

Note: "Excellent."

• • • • •

Middle Creek Goose Breast

> 1 skinned goose breast
> Soft butter
> Hunt Sauce (see "Game Sauces" chapter)

Begin making Hunt Sauce. Then fillet the meat from both sides of the goose breast bone with a thin, flexible knife, scraping the bone to get all the meat. Place the two fillets on a buttered piece of foil on a broiler pan. Generously spread soft butter over the fillets. Place in a preheated broiler about 4 inches from the heat. Broil 5 minutes on each side (10 minutes total broiling time). While the meat is cooking, finish preparing the Hunt Sauce. Place the broiled fillets on a wooden carving board and cut into *paper-thin* slices. Serve immediately, ladled with Hunt Sauce. Serves 4 generously, 6 adequately.

Note: "Delicious."

• • • • •

Goose Liver Pâté

1 pound goose livers
¼ cup minced onion
2 tablespoons butter
¼ cup ripe olive juice
1 teaspoon steak sauce
¼ cup minced ripe olives
¼ cup heavy cream
¼ cup cognac or brandy
¼ cup softened butter
1 tablespoon minced parsley
Salt & pepper to taste

Fry the onion in 2 tablespoons of butter over medium heat until limp—about 5 minutes. Add olive juice, steak sauce, and goose livers to pan. Cover pan and cook over low heat until the livers are tender, about 10 to 15 minutes. Cool for 10 minutes. Puree mixture in a blender or food processor with ripe olives, cream, cognac, and ¼ cup butter. Blend well. Add parsley, salt and pepper, and blend. Pour into a serving dish and chill until ready to serve with bland crackers.

Note: "Marvelous."

• • • • •

Pickled Goose Hearts

Goose hearts
2 whole cloves
2 bay leaves
1 small onion sliced
⅓ cup wine vinegar
⅔ cup cold water

Put hearts, cloves, and bay leaves in a large saucepan with enough water to cover meat. Bring the water to a boil, cover, turn heat down, and simmer until the hearts are tender, about 35 minutes. Cool and slice the hearts thinly. Place in a glass bowl with the onion and add the vinegar and water. Add more water, if necessary to cover the meat. Cover and marinate in the refrigerator for 24 hours. Add a little salt and pepper if necessary. Drain, pat slices dry with paper towels, and serve on crackers or rye bread or as finger food.

Note: "Great appetizers."

• • • • •

To prepare tough (or uncooked) goose legs, wings, and backbone for the next two recipes, cut them into manageable pieces with game shears. Put them in a big pot with enough water to cover the meat and bones, a bay leaf, and a dash of salt and pepper. Bring the water to a boil, reduce the heat to simmer, cover, and cook until the meat is fork-tender. (Time depends on the age of the goose.) Remove the meat from the broth, cool, and cut into bite-size pieces. Save the broth for the last recipe or a soup in the "Odds & Ends" chapter.

Delaware Valley Goose

> 2 cups cooked goose meat (bite-size pieces)
> 3 tablespoons butter
> $\frac{1}{4}$ cup finely chopped onions
> $\frac{1}{2}$ cup sliced mushrooms
> 3 tablespoons flour
> 1 tablespoon tomato paste
> 1 tablespoon steak sauce
> $1\frac{1}{2}$ cups light cream
> Salt & pepper
> Dash Tabasco sauce
> Hot cooked spaghetti
> Parmesan cheese

Heat the butter in a large skillet and fry the onions and mushrooms for about 7 minutes over medium-high heat. Stir in flour.

Add tomato paste and steak sauce. Stirring constantly, add the cream slowly. Heat and stir until the sauce is thick. Add Tabasco and goose meat, mix, and heat, sprinkling with a little salt and pepper. Cook spaghetti according to directions, drain and wash in very hot water. Drain again and add to the skillet and toss with sauce over low heat until thoroughly heated. Serve on a heated platter, sprinkling generously with cheese. Serves 4.

Note: "Very good."

• • • • •

Creamy Goose Sauce

        2 cups cooked goose meat (bite-size chunks)
        ½ cup chopped onion
        ¾ cup chopped celery
        ¼ cup chopped green pepper
        3 tablespoons butter
        3 tablespoons flour
       1½ cups goose broth
        6 drops Tabasco sauce
        2 egg yolks, beaten
        3 tablespoons white wine
           Salt & pepper
           Parsley sprigs

Fry the onion, celery, and green pepper in the butter until tender, about 7 to 10 minutes. Add flour and gradually add the broth, stirring constantly. Add Tabasco and remove the pan from the heat. Add a little of the sauce to the egg yolks and blend. Return the mixture to the pan and stir in immediately. Add wine and goose meat. Salt and pepper to taste and heat until bubbling hot. Serve on hot buttered rice or toast. Garnish with parsley. Serves 4.

Note: "Great."

• • • • •

Small Game

Cooking small game can be a problem because it's difficult to determine the age of the animal. A young rabbit, for instance, can be tender after 45 minutes of cooking; a two-year-old may take $1\frac{1}{2}$ hours. The solution is to start dinner early if you suspect an old-timer is in the pot. If it's tender sooner than you guessed, simply turn the heat to low (or entirely off) until dinner time. With the moist-cooking methods, no harm is done. When the animal is parboiled before the final browning, the initial cooking can be done an hour or so early with the final frying done at the last minute. When cooking squirrels (three animals for four servings), there may be a grey-beard in the pot with a couple young ones. Then, simply remove the meat pieces as they tenderize and allow the tough ones to cook longer.

At times you can spot an older animal; they may be bigger, tougher to skin and have the "general appearance" of an old-timer—the wear and tear shows. These animals should be labeled as such when they are frozen. Then cooking time can be adjusted for them. For best results, try to cook equal aged animals together. Lucky for the cook, most rabbits and squirrels don't live long enough in the wild (even if not hunted) to become too tough.

Small game should be gutted in the field if a long day of hunting is ahead. Bury the entrails under a rock if possible since hunting dogs can pick up tapeworms from some animal entrails. If the animal hasn't been gutted in the field it is better to skin it first. Chop the head (and squirrel tail) off with a heavy hunting knife. Cut a slit in the middle of the back skin; insert your fingers in both sides of the slit and pull in opposite directions with even pressure until the skin is over the first joint on all legs. With luck and proper pressure, the skin will slip down the front and back legs at the same time. Sever the legs at the joint. It's easier to skin warm animals than cold ones.

Most recipes call for small game to be cut into five serving pieces—four legs and the backstrap. Again, use a sharp, stout knife. There is no need to soak small game. Wash briefly but thoroughly under cold running water, probing with a sharp knife to remove shot, bone chips, and blood clots. Blot with paper towels and store either in the refrigerator (up to two days) or in the freezer. Before freezing, double wrap the game in plastic or aluminum wrap and then good quality freezer paper. Label as to species, number of servings, age (if known), and date. Most well-wrapped small game can be stored in a good (see introduction) freezer for four to six months.

RABBIT

As everyone knows, rabbits are prolific animals. As a result, there are usually plenty of tender, young targets for fall gunners. In years past, the disease tularemia was a worry to those who hunted rabbits since it is easily transmitted from animal to human. Because of modern drugs, serious cases of tularemia are nearly nonexistent. If your conservation agency has reported any local outbreaks, a good precaution is to wear rubber gloves while cleaning rabbits. Thorough cooking eliminates all danger to diners.

It has long been traditional to cook rabbit to the well-done stage. The recipes in this section reflect this preference. However, a growing number of cooks feel that the tender backstrap meat is over cooked with these methods. If you would like to try a special treat, fillet the meat from each side of the backbone into long strips, scraping the knife along the bone. Roll the thin loins in flour seasoned with a dash of salt and pepper. Heat a couple tablespoons of butter and cooking oil in a heavy skillet over medium-high heat and fry the meat for a minute or two on all sides, about 6 minutes total cooking time. The meat should be tender and juicy and just past the pink stage. Try this only in areas which are tularemia-free. Save the rest of the rabbit for the other recipes in this chapter.

One rabbit will usually serve three adults. It can be stretched into four servings by offering a soup course or extra vegetable dishes with the meal.

While the flavor of wild rabbit isn't quite as mild as the domestic varieties, it can easily be overpowered by an intense wine. For simple fried or braised recipes, a Beaujolais with a fresh, grapy tang will usually be right. If you like the sweeter, softer German wines, Moselle or Rhine will also be fine and some of the slightly dry California Rieslings may be best of all. With a cooking treatment that calls for tomato sauce or extra spices, a somewhat more pungent wine would suit better—an Italian Bardolino or a California Zinfandel. Beer can be served with recipes that use it in the cooking method.

Recipe Notes:

Special Fried Rabbit—young animal works well—preparation time, about 15 minutes—lovely, mild orange flavor.

Riverside Rabbit—good recipe for older animal—preparation time, about 25 minutes—spicy flavor.

Ruffed Creek Rabbit—any age animal—preparation time, about 25 minutes—rich, creamy tomato taste.

Piney Creek Rabbit—especially suitable for older animal—preparation time, about 25 minutes—delightful creamy taste.

Braised Rabbit—any age animal—preparation time, about 35 minutes—rich and spicy stew.

Clear Ridge Rabbit—any age animal—preparation time, about 30 minutes—intense flavor, creamy dish.

Special Fried Rabbit

> 1 rabbit, cut into serving pieces
> ⅓ cup flour
> Salt & pepper
> 1 tablespoon cooking oil
> 2 tablespoons butter
> ¼ teaspoon thyme
> ⅓ cup orange juice
> ⅓ cup water

Place flour with a little salt and pepper in a paper bag. Add the rabbit pieces and shake well to coat them with the flour mixture. Heat the oil and butter in a frying pan until very hot. Add rabbit and brown on all sides, turning with tongs. Sprinkle the pieces with thyme, add orange juice and water to the pan, cover, and turn heat to high simmer. Cook about 1 to 1½ hours, until the rabbit is tender when a fork is inserted in the leg meat. Watch the liquid level carefully, adding more water if necessary. Serve with pan sauce ladled over each piece. Serves 3.

Note: "Jim's favorite rabbit recipe."

• • • • •

Riverside Rabbit

> 1 rabbit, cut into serving pieces
> 16 ounces beer
> 1 garlic clove, minced
> 1 bay leaf
> 1 onion, sliced
> 5 whole cloves
> ¼ cup flour
> Salt & pepper
> ¼ cup cooking oil
> Quick Mixing flour

Place rabbit, beer, garlic, bay leaf, onion, and cloves in a nonmetal casserole or glass bowl, cover, and marinate in the refrigerator for 24 hours. Dry the rabbit pieces on paper towels. Place flour, salt, and pepper (just a little of each) in a paper bag with rabbit. Shake well to coat rabbit. Heat oil in a heavy skillet and brown rabbit on all sides. Add marinade to pan, cover, and simmer for 1 to 2 hours, until the meat is fork-tender. Young animals will take only one hour, while older ones require more time. Thicken the sauce with Quick Mixing flour and serve over rabbit. Serves 3.

Note: "Excellent."

• • • • •

Ruffed Creek Rabbit

> 1 rabbit, cut into serving pieces
> Seasoned flour
> 3 tablespoons cooking oil
> 1 large onion, sliced
> 1 cup beef bouillon
> 1 cup chopped tomatoes (seeded)
> $\frac{1}{4}$ teaspoon dillweed
> 1 teaspoon minced parsley
> $\frac{1}{3}$ cup sour cream
> Paprika
> Parsley sprigs
> Noodles

Douse rabbit pieces in flour that has been seasoned with a little salt and pepper and brown on all sides in the hot oil in a large skillet. Fry the onion slices at the same time in the skillet. When the rabbit is brown, add bouillon, tomatoes, dillweed, and parsley and stir well. (Remove seeds from fresh tomatoes with your index finger, scraping the juicy sections.) Cover and simmer until the rabbit is tender, about 1½ hours. When the meat is done, transfer to a heated platter and keep warm in a 150°F. oven. Stir the sour cream into the pan juices and serve in a gravy boat. Ladle juices amply over hot, buttered noodles and rabbit pieces. Garnish dish with parsley sprigs and a sprinkle of paprika. Serves 3.

Note: "Very good."

• • • • •

Piney Creek Rabbit

> 1 rabbit, cut into serving pieces
> Water to cover
> 1 onion, diced
> 1 celery rib top with leaves, diced
> ½ teaspoon salt
> ¼ teaspoon ground pepper
> 1 teaspoon crushed rosemary
> ½ cup dry white wine
> ½ cup sour cream
> ½ teaspoon lemon rind
> ½ teaspoon marjoram
> 3 tablespoons chopped parsley
> Quick Mixing flour

Place rabbit in a large pot with water, onion, celery, salt, pepper, rosemary, and wine. Bring to a boil, cover, and simmer until the rabbit is fork-tender. With a young rabbit this could be 45 minutes; an older one will take longer—up to 2 hours. When done, remove the rabbit from the pot and turn the heat to high. Reduce the broth to 1½ cups. Lower heat and thicken the broth by sprinkling Quick Mixing flour into it, stirring constantly until it is the consistency of gravy. (The dish may be held at this point for an hour or so.) Add sour cream, lemon rind, and marjoram and stir. Return the rabbit to the pan and reheat. Serve rabbit with a generous dollop of gravy ladled over each piece and some parsley sprinkled on top. Serve the rest of the gravy in a sauce boat to be ladled over hot rice, noodles, or potatoes. Serves 3.

Note: "Very good."

•　•　•　•　•

Braised Rabbit

    1 rabbit, cut into serving pieces
      Flour
      Salt & pepper
    3 tablespoons cooking oil
    1 onion, sliced
    1 cup beer
    $\frac{1}{3}$ cup chili sauce
    1 tablespoon brown sugar
    $\frac{1}{8}$ teaspoon garlic powder
    $\frac{1}{4}$ cup water
    3 medium potatoes, quartered
    3 carrots, cut into 2-inch chunks
      Quick Mixing flour

Place about $\frac{1}{4}$ cup flour on a piece of waxed paper and mix a little salt and pepper with it. Roll the rabbit pieces in it and brown in a heavy skillet in hot oil. Brown on all sides. Add the onion and brown with the rabbit. Place the beer, chili sauce, sugar, garlic, and water in a large jar and shake until mixed. Pour the mixture over the browned rabbit. Cover, bring to a boil, lower heat to high simmer, and cook for $\frac{3}{4}$ hour to $1\frac{1}{4}$ hours until the rabbit starts to tenderize. Time depends on age of rabbit. Turn rabbit in the juice and add potatoes and carrots. Cover and cook another $\frac{3}{4}$ hour until all is tender. Remove the rabbit and vegetables to a heated platter and place in a 150°F. oven. Sprinkle the pan juices with flour, stir, and boil until the juices are a little thick. Serve in a gravy boat to be ladled over meat and vegetables. Serves 3.

Note: "Great."

• • • • •

Clear Ridge Rabbit

1 rabbit, cut into serving pieces
Flour seasoned with salt & pepper
2 tablespoons cooking oil
2 tablespoons butter
1 small onion, finely chopped
1 cup chopped mushrooms
1 tablespoon Dijon-style mustard
2 tablespoons flour
1½ cups light cream
¼ cup cognac or brandy
Salt & pepper
1 tablespoon chopped parsley

Douse rabbit pieces in flour mixture. Brown on all sides in a mixture of oil and butter heated in a large skillet. Place the browned rabbit in a casserole dish. Add onion and mushrooms to the skillet. Cook for 5 minutes, stirring, until they are limp. Stir the 2 tablespoons of flour into the vegetables. Add the cream and cognac to the pan slowly, stirring constantly until the sauce thickens slightly. Add salt and pepper to taste. Brush the rabbit pieces with mustard and pour the hot sauce over them. Cover and place in a preheated 350°F. oven for 1 to 2 hours, depending on the age of the rabbit. Sprinkle the cooked meat with chopped parsley and serve with hot, buttered noodles. Spoon some of the sauce over the noodles. Serves 3.

Note: "Excellent."

• • • • •

SQUIRREL

Squirrels live a little longer in the wild than rabbits so it's easier to have an old bushy-tail in the pot, especially when it takes three of the little animals to serve four adults. Start the meal early if you suspect a grey-beard is to be cooked. (Refer to the lead-in to this chapter for tips on aging small game animals.)

Because of their small size, squirrel is more likely to become freezer burned than other meat. The best way to prevent this is to freeze squirrel pieces in a plastic container filled with water. Seal the lid with tape and all will be well in a freezer for six months. If there is an extra squirrel left in the freezer at the end of hunting season, use it in one of the recipes in the "Odds & Ends" chapter.

Note: Some rabbit recipes are also excellent with squirrel. Try "Riverside Rabbit" or "Piney Creek Rabbit," remembering to cook three squirrels for four servings.

Squirrel is one of my favorite wild meats. The flavor is mild yet distinctive and can be fixed in a wide variety of methods and still taste like squirrel. Here again, California Zinfandel is my preference. Some of the vintage Zinfandels are exquisite but many of the jug labels are equally satisfying.

A well-aged Pinot Noir from France will also do perfectly (a young Burgundy can be a bit mean in taste but will soften well in about five or six years). A California jug Burgundy is almost always ready for drinking when purchased and might be preferred over Zinfandel if you object to the spicy taste of that grape.

There may be a white wine somewhere in the world that blends well with squirrel—but I haven't found it yet.

Recipe Notes:

Woodlot Squirrel—good with young animals—preparation time, about 20 minutes—light, delicately flavored dish.

Buckhorn Squirrel—good for older animals—preparation time, about 15 minutes—rich flavor.

Spring Grove Squirrel—any age animals—preparation time, about 45 minutes—pleasant, orange-flavored meat.

Creamed Squirrel—especially good with older animals—preparation time, about 35 minutes—lightly spiced, creamy flavor; great for those who like their meat boneless.

Woodlot Squirrel

> 3 squirrels, cut into pieces
> 1 egg
> Fine bread crumbs
> 2 tablespoons butter or margarine
> 2 tablespoons cooking oil
> $\frac{1}{2}$ cup white wine
> $\frac{1}{2}$ cup orange juice
> Pepper to taste

Dry squirrel pieces on paper towels. Beat egg thoroughly. Dip squirrel in the beaten egg and then roll in bread crumbs. (I used flavored bread crumbs. If you don't, add a little garlic and onion salt and minced parsley and mix well.) Brown squirrel on all sides in hot butter and oil in a large frying pan over medium-high heat. Add wine and orange juice to the pan, cover, and turn the heat to simmer. Cook until all the pieces are fork-tender—45 minutes to 1 hour for young squirrels. Turn pieces once during the cooking. Serve with orange wedges. Serves 4.

Note: "Excellent."

• • • • •

Buckhorn Squirrel

> 3 squirrels, cut into pieces
> Water to cover
> 2 bay leaves
> Seasoned flour
> 4 tablespoons butter
> $\frac{3}{4}$ cup stewing liquid
> $\frac{3}{4}$ cup dry red wine
> 1 beef bouillon cube
> Pinch of chili powder
> 1 cup whole mushrooms

Place squirrel in a large pot with water and bay leaves. Simmer until all the pieces are done. Young squirrels will tenderize quicker than old ones. Remove any pieces of meat that are tender and reserve until all are done. Drain the meat on paper towels and save $\frac{3}{4}$ cup of the stewing liquid. (This part of the recipe can be completed an hour or so before dinner if you wish.)

Roll the squirrel pieces in flour that has been seasoned with a little salt and pepper. Heat the butter in a heavy skillet and brown the squirrel over medium-high heat. Add the rest of the ingredients—stewing liquid, red wine, bouillon cube, chili powder, and mushrooms, cover, and simmer for 20 minutes. Serves 4.

Note: "Very good."

• • • • •

Spring Grove Squirrel

    3 squirrels, cut into serving pieces
    1 onion
    1 celery top with leaves
    1 beef bouillon cube
      Salt & pepper
      Flour
      Kitchen Bouquet
    3 tablespoons butter
    $\frac{1}{2}$ teaspoon curry powder
    $\frac{1}{3}$ cup fresh orange juice
    $\frac{1}{4}$ teaspoon grated orange peel
    1 tablespoon cornstarch
      Parsley sprigs

Place squirrel pieces, onion, celery, and bouillon cube in a pot with enough water to cover the squirrel. Add a little salt and pepper. Bring to a boil, lower heat, and simmer until all the squirrel pieces are tender. Remove the pieces as they are done and reserve. Cook the broth down to 1 cup; thicken with some Quick Mixing flour, adding a little Kitchen Bouquet to darken the gravy.

Roll the meat in flour and brown on all sides in the butter in a large skillet over high heat. Sprinkle the squirrel with curry. Mix the orange juice, peel, and cornstarch thoroughly. Spoon a little of the mixture over each piece of squirrel and toss the pieces in the hot frying pan for a couple minutes, adding more butter to the pan if necessary. Serve with hot buttered rice with the gravy ladled over it. Garnish with parsley. Serves 4.

Note: "Great recipe."

• • • • •

Creamed Squirrel

3 squirrels, cut into pieces
Flour seasoned with salt & pepper
$\frac{1}{4}$ cup cooking oil
1 onion, chopped
$\frac{1}{2}$ cup chopped mushrooms
1 cup dry white wine
$\frac{1}{2}$ teaspoon thyme
1 tablespoon chopped parsley
1 cup light cream
Quick Mixing flour

Roll the squirrel in flour mixture. Heat cooking oil in a large, heavy skillet and fry squirrel on all sides until brown. Remove the pieces from the pan. Fry onion and mushrooms in the skillet over medium-high heat for 5 minutes and return squirrel to the skillet. Add wine, thyme, and parsley to pan; mix well, cover, and simmer until squirrel is tender, 1 to 1$\frac{1}{2}$ hours. Add water to pan if necessary. Remove squirrel from pan and cool. (This part of the recipe can be completed an hour or so before dinner, if you wish.)

Remove meat from the bones. Add enough water to pan liquid to make 1 cup. Add cream to the pan and bring to the boiling point. If the liquid is too thin, add a little flour and stir to thicken. Add pieces of meat, heat, and serve over toast or hot biscuits. Garnish with parsley. Serves 4 or 5.

Note: "Delicious."

• • • • •

WOODCHUCK

When you consider all the good things that make up the diet of woodchucks (or groundhogs, if you prefer), it's no wonder they are good to eat. Naturally, young ones are more tender than the old-timers.

Skinning woodchucks is easier if it is done while the chuck is still warm. Use the same technique as with rabbits and squirrels (see the lead-in to the "Small Game" section). Because the bones are larger, use a small hatchet with a chopping block to lop off the head and feet. Save the tail of an adult chuck for your favorite fly tyer. The backstrap can be cut into two or three serving pieces, the legs should be left whole, and the odd-looking shoulder pieces can be discarded since there is very little meat on them.

A young animal will average 4 to 6 pounds when skinned and cleaned; an older one may be twice as heavy. Plan on one pound per serving.

Woodchuck is a rich-tasting meat but not strong. Several different red wines are fine with most recipes, such as Burgundy, Zinfandel, Merlot, and Petite Sirah. If you want to drink the king of the red wines with woodchuck, go ahead and try a bottle of Cabernet Sauvignon. The meat might not sound like royal fare to some, but the Cabernet Sauvignon wine will taste perfect with it. All Cabernet is not outrageously expensive. A good, well-aged bottle can be had for under $7 at this writing and there are even some jug wines that contain enough of the grape to be called Cabernet Sauvignon on the label.

Few white wines would stand up to woodchuck, so don't bother with them, but don't overlook a good bottle of imported beer of the dark persuasion or a snappy bottle of ale. One of the greatest woodchuck meals I ever ate was stew with a couple bottles of Canadian Moosehead Ale.

If you try the Italian-Style Braised Woodchuck recipe, by all means buy a bottle of Italian Classico Chianti. Terrific!

Recipe Notes:

Fried Woodchuck—older animal—preparation time, about 10 minutes—pleasant, light flavor.

Woodchuck Stew—young animal—preparation time, about 30 minutes—hearty, filling dish.

Italian-Style Braised Woodchuck—any age animal—preparation time, about 40 minutes—rich, spicy flavor.

Fried Woodchuck

> 1 woodchuck, cut into serving pieces
> Flour
> ¼ cup cooking oil
> Pepper
> ½ teaspoon marjoram
> 1 cup water
> 1 beef bouillon cube

Roll the woodchuck pieces in flour. Heat the cooking oil in a large, heavy skillet and brown the woodchuck on all sides over medium-high heat. Sprinkle the woodchuck with a little pepper and the marjoram. Add a cup of water and the bouillon to the skillet, bring to a boil, lower the heat to simmer, cover, and cook for 1½ to 2½ hours, until the pieces are very tender. Add more water to the pan, if necessary. Thicken the pan juices with Quick Mixing flour, if you wish. Serves 4 to 8, depending on the size of the woodchuck.

Note: "Good."

• • • •

Woodchuck Stew

> 1 young woodchuck, cut into serving pieces
> Flour seasoned with salt & pepper
> ¼ cup cooking oil
> 1 garlic clove, minced
> 4 onions
> 4 potatoes, cut into chunks
> 4 carrots, cut into chunks
> 1 cup chicken stock
> 1 cup hot water

Heat cooking oil in a Dutch oven. Roll woodchuck pieces in flour that has been mixed with a little salt and pepper. Brown the meat on all sides in the Dutch oven. Add the garlic, onions, potatoes, carrots, stock, and water to the pan. Sprinkle with a little salt and pepper. Bring the liquid to a boil on top of the stove. Cover and place in a preheated 350°F. oven for 1½ to 2 hours, until the meat is fork-tender. Serves 4 to 6. The pan juices may be thickened with Quick Mixing flour to serve with the meat and vegetables.

Note: "Very good."

•　•　•　•　•

Italian-Style Braised Woodchuck

    1 woodchuck, cut into serving pieces
    1 cup sugar
    ¼ cup vinegar
    ¼ cup salt
    2 bay leaves
    1 slice onion
    ¼ teaspoon chili powder
    1 quart water
    Flour
    ¼ cup cooking oil
    1 chopped onion
    1 chopped carrot
    1 chopped rib of celery with leaves
    1 cup tomato juice
    6 oz. tomato paste
    ½ teaspoon oregano
    ½ teaspoon basil
    ½ teaspoon marjoram
    Cooked noodles
    Parsley sprigs

Put water, sugar, vinegar, salt, bay leaves, onion slice, and chili powder in a large saucepan and bring to a boil. Lower heat and simmer for 10 minutes. Allow the mixture to cool to room temperature. Place woodchuck pieces in a nonmetal dish or bowl and pour the cooled marinade mixture over it. Add more water if necessary to cover meat. Cover and put in the refrigerator for 48 hours.

Remove meat from the marinade and dry on paper towels. Roll the pieces in flour. Heat the oil in a large, heavy skillet and brown the meat on all sides. Add the chopped onion, carrot, and celery to the pan, along with the tomato juice, tomato paste, oregano, basil, and marjoram. Stir, bring to a boil, cover, and lower heat to simmer. Cook until the meat is tender $1\frac{1}{2}$ to $2\frac{1}{2}$ hours, depending on the age of the woodchuck. Serve on a heated platter surrounding a bed of buttered noodles. Pour a little of the sauce over both meat and noodles. Serve with a green salad and hot Italian bread. Serves 4 to 8.

Note: "Excellent."

• • • • •

Big Game

Deer, moose, antelope, caribou, and elk generally require the same type of recipes. They all have fine textured meat but don't have much natural fat. Do not use recipes that are structured for domestic animals. Most wild animals should be cooked hot and fast or long and slow. These are the only methods that work well. Try the medium route and you'll fail; the meat will be tough and dry.

The taste of these animals will vary because they are opportunists. If their preferred diet is in short supply, they will eat what is available. Another factor which will affect the tenderness and taste of these animals is totally controlled by the hunter. If he or she makes a sure, swift-killing shot, the meat will be unaffected by adrenalin. An animal that travels for a considerable distance after being hit will definitely be tougher than one that is dropped with a single, deadly shot. Careful cleaning and transportation of the big-game animal also has a big part to play in the final flavor of the meat. Take your time, do it right. If the stomach or intestines were pierced by a bullet or in the cleaning, wash the exposed flesh *thoroughly* with cold water as soon as possible. Remove (and discard) the bruised area around the bullet entry and exit area. Carry a couple of plastic bags for the heart and liver. They are worth the extra effort; the flavor is excellent and they are packed with nutrition. Treat the animal as carefully as you would prime beef. By any yardstick, it is more valuable than the best meat you can buy.

Separate your animal into several cuts, trimming off all natural fat. There are a multitude of recipes you'll want to try so your family doesn't get bored with wild meat. I've known hunters who have their whole animal ground into burger. Just how much venison or moose or antelope burger can one eat? And think what you are missing—all those wonderful chops, steaks, roasts, and stews.

I mentioned earlier that the taste of these animals is affected by what they eat. For instance, in my home state of Pennsylvania the flavor of venison harvested in the north central, forested part of the state is markedly different from those bagged in the farm country 200 miles to the south. The former have practically eaten themselves out of house and home and subside at times on what is considered poverty rations. There aren't as many deer in southern Pennsylvania but they are well fed, fat, and much tastier in the pot.

A great test is to broil some chops to the medium-rare stage. If they are succulent and tender, the entire animal will be the same (if you follow good recipes). If the flavor is a little less than satisfactory, you'll want to look for recipes that call for a few herbs and spices in the cooking process. I'm betting that 90% of the time, the chops will be absolutely great!

I can think of no better time to crack a bottle of Cabernet Sauvignon than with a platter of medium-rare venison chops or a loin roast. The same goes for top-round steak from deer, moose, elk, antelope, or caribou. And just because the grape that particular wine is made from has a fancy sounding name doesn't mean that good Cabernet (or Bordeaux or Claret as it is sometimes called) has to wear a fancy price. If your budget can stand it once in a while, you might indulge yourself and try a bottle of one of the really great ones—such as Chateau Latour, Chateau Margaux or Lafite-Rothschild. Even a young one, less than six years old, will command a hefty price tag, but you might want to find out what all the fuss is about.

There are some excellent wines that come from areas bordering on the lands of the great ones that are as pleasant to drink and cost about one-fourth the price, say from $6.00 to $15.00. There are dozens of them and rather than recommend a specific one, ask your wine dealer to suggest a good "little chateau" Cabernet. He'll try to steer you right because he'd like a new customer.

The California Cabernets get better all the time and for my money, rival the best France has to offer. The Robert Mondavi label is one to count on, and it's available in most states. Beaulieu, Louis Martini, and Concannon are three more of my favorites. A bit less expensive but still excellent buys are Cabernet Sauvignons from Almaden, Inglenook, Christian Brothers, Krug, and Fetzer.

One of the outstanding values in Cabernet wine these days is found behind the Premiat label. This wine is imported from Romania and can be had in most stores for under $4.00. It's the real thing with lots of aromatic goodness and the slight, acidy bite a good Cabernet should have. If you see it in your store, buy a case at the current low price. It's bound to go up soon.

With venison liver, stews, and combination dishes that feature heavy sauces, the rich taste of a real Burgundy or wine made from Pinot Noir grapes is a fine choice. The best of the French wines for venison are the Cotes du Rhones. There isn't anything made in this country that is quite like them but we're coming close. A few California makers are bottling wines made from pure or almost pure Merlot grapes (which are used as a blending wine in some Cabernets) that are superb venison wines and especially so with well-done entrees.

If you're still in doubt and are not sure you might like the headier wines, stick with our old trustworthy American Zinfandel or a Petite Sirah.

If all fails and no wine is at hand or you choose not to drink it, a cold bottle of imported beer or ale—one of the dark ones— or a premium American beer will not taste all that bad either. Under no circumstances should you drink a light, white wine with venison. It just doesn't blend well. It's kind of like having a dill pickle with chocolate ice cream!

ROASTS

A roast from the loin area should always be cooked to the medium-rare stage, a hind-quarter roast can be either well done or medium rare, depending on how old the animal is (youngsters are usually more tender). A front shoulder roast is best prepared by a long-cooking method since the meat tends to be a bit on the chewy side. Shoulder meat is also excellent as stew meat. Check the "Smoking Game" chapter for an easy, venison-ham recipe.

Recipe Notes:

Easter Rump Roast—roast from a young animal—preparation time, about 10 minutes—medium rare, delicate flavor.

Middle Creek Roast—top round roast from any age animal— preparation time, about 30 minutes—hearty, delicious meal.

Creamy Rump Roast—large roast, good recipe for older animal—preparation time, about 15 minutes—rich, creamy flavor.

Warriors Mark Roast—shoulder roast from any age animal— preparation time, about 35 minutes—spicy, pungent dish.

Black Forest Roast—loin roast, especially good with young animal—preparation time, about 5 minutes—medium-rare meat, pure flavor.

Prouty Run Roast—shoulder roast from any age animal—preparation time, about 15 minutes—hearty flavor.

Easter Rump Roast

$3\frac{3}{4}$- to 4-pound rump roast (young animal)
1 garlic clove, slivered
$\frac{1}{4}$ teaspoon rosemary
  Cooking oil

Cut slits in top of roast and insert small sliver of garlic and rosemary into the slits. Rub the roast with cooking oil and let sit for 1 hour at room temperature. Place the roast in a baking dish. Roast in a preheated 450°F. oven for 15 minutes. Lower heat to 350°F. and roast another $1\frac{1}{4}$ hours. The roast should be uncovered the entire roasting time. If you use a meat thermometer, it should register 155°F. for medium rare. If your roast is larger or smaller, roast for about 18 minutes per pound at the 350°F. oven temperature. Let the roast sit on a heated platter for 5 minutes before carving. Make gravy from the pan drippings if you wish. (I pre-

pared this roast just like my Easter leg of lamb; hence the name.)
Serves 4 to 6.

Note: "Super."

. . . . .

Middle Creek Roast

> 3- pound top round roast
> Flour
> 2 tablespoons cooking oil
> Pepper
> 1 garlic clove
> 1 envelope onion-mushroom soup mix
> 5 large carrots, cut in bite-size chunks
> 5 potatoes with skin, scrubbed and quartered
> 1 tablespoon cornstarch

Roll roast in flour. Heat oil in a Dutch oven and brown the
roast on all sides over medium-high heat. Amply sprinkle roast
with pepper. Add garlic and contents of the soup envelope to pot
along with 2 cups of hot water. Cover pot and simmer until meat
is nearly tender, for $1\frac{1}{2}$ to 2 hours. Turn roast a couple times during
the cooking. Add vegetables and simmer another 30 minutes.
Remove meat and vegetables to a heated platter. Thicken sauce
with the cornstarch dissolved in $\frac{1}{2}$ cup cold water. Stir and heat
until gravy is thick. Serve garnished with parsley sprigs. Serves 4 to 5.

Note: "Excellent."

. . . . .

Creamy Rump Roast

    6-pound rump roast
    1 can cream of mushroom soup
    2 garlic cloves, slivered
    ½ cup dry red wine
    ½ teaspoon basil
    Salt & pepper

    Insert garlic slivers in slits cut in roast with the tip of a sharp knife. Place the roast in a roasting pan. Pour the soup (undiluted) over the roast, along with the wine. Sprinkle the roast with basil and a little salt and pepper. Cover and roast in a preheated 350°F. oven for 2½ to 3½ hours (2½ for a 6-pound roast from a young animal—3½ from older or larger meat). Baste twice with pan juices during the roasting time. Serve the roast with pan juices ladled over thin slices. Will serve 6 to 8.

Note: "Very good."

• • • • •

Warriors Mark Roast

    4-pound shoulder roast
    Flour seasoned with salt & pepper
    3 tablespoons cooking oil
    1 onion, sliced
    ½ green pepper, chopped
    2 garlic cloves, minced
    1 1-pound can tomatoes
    ½ cup port wine
    ½ teaspoon thyme
    1 parsley sprig
    2 whole cloves
   10 peppercorns
    1 bay leaf, crumbled

Roll the roast in the flour mixture. Heat the oil in a Dutch oven and brown the roast over medium-high heat. When brown, remove the roast from the pot. Fry the onions, green pepper, and garlic for 5 minutes, stirring often. Add tomatoes, port, and thyme to the pot and heat. Place the parsley, cloves, peppercorn, and bay leaf on a double piece of cheesecloth and tie with string into a bag. Add the bag to the pot and stir. When the mixture is boiling, add the roast and baste with the sauce. Cover and place in a preheated 350°F. oven. Roast for about 2½ hours, or until tender. Baste several times with pan juices during the roasting. Slice thinly and serve with pan juices. Will serve 4. (Shoulder roasts are difficult to slice because of the bones; do the best you can.)

Note: "Excellent sauce—a real hit!"

•   •   •   •   •

Black Forest Roast

> 1½- to 2-pound loin roast
> Soft butter
> ¼ teaspoon thyme
> Dash of garlic powder

Have roast at room temperature. Rub it with butter and sprinkle with thyme and garlic powder. Place in a roasting pan. Preheat the oven to 450°F. Put the roast in the oven and cook for 15 minutes. Turn the oven to 400°F. and roast another 15 to 25 minutes; time depends on the thickness of the roast (yearling venison roast would require the minimum time). Cut the meat into thin slices and serve as is or with Mushroom Game Sauce (see "Game Sauces" chapter). Serves 4.

Note: "Great."

•   •   •   •   •

Prouty Run Roast

> 5-pound shoulder roast
> 1 teaspoon marjoram
> 1 onion, sliced
> 1 rib celery, chopped
> 1 carrot, sliced
> 1 bay leaf
> 8 ounces beer
> Quick Mixing flour

Sprinkle the roast with the marjoram. Place the onion, celery, and carrot on the bottom of an oven cooking bag. Add the roast, bay leaf, and beer. Close the bag according to manufacturer's directions and place in a roasting pan. Preheat the oven to 350°F. and roast the meat for 2 to 2½ hours, until tender. Thicken pan juices with flour and serve with the roast. Serves 4 to 6.

Note: "Good."

•　•　•　•　•

CHOPS & STEAKS

Chops and steaks should be cut ¾ to 1 inch thick for most of my recipes. If they are cut thinner, you'll have to reduce frying and broiling time and they won't be as tender and juicy, especially those cooked to the medium-rare stage.

Chops should *always* be cooked medium rare. If you don't like your meat prepared this way, give your chops to a friend who does. Steak can be cooked hot and fast, or long and slow; there are recipes for both. For hearty appetites, serve ½ pound of meat per person.

Recipe Notes:

Broiled Chops—1-inch thick meat—preparation time, about 5 minutes (doesn't include sauce)—medium rare, pure flavor.

Fried Chops—1-inch thick chops—preparation time, about 15 minutes—juicy and delicious.

Broiled Steak—1-inch thick meat—preparation time, about 5 minutes—medium rare, simple and pure dish.

Buck Valley Steak—1-inch thick steak—preparation time, about 20 minutes—light, delicate steak flavor.

Juicy Cheese Steak—$\frac{1}{2}$- to 1-inch thick steak—preparation time, about 20 minutes—sturdy, Italian-style flavor.

Les's Swiss Steak—especially good with older animal; $\frac{1}{2}$- to 1-inch steaks—preparation time, about 25 minutes—spicy dish for those who like the well-done treatment.

Rolled Steak—good with thin steak ($\frac{1}{2}$ inch)—preparation time, about 35 minutes—hearty meal.

Venison Shish Kebab—1-inch thick meat—preparation time, about 30 minutes—flavorful meal, everything will be tender but crisp.

Broiled Chops

> $1\frac{1}{2}$ to 2 pounds chops, about 1 inch thick
> Soft butter
> $\frac{1}{8}$ teaspoon marjoram
> Salt & pepper

Spread chops on both sides with soft butter and sprinkle with marjoram. Place them on a broiler pan and put under a preheated broiler, 4 inches from the heat. Broil 4 to 5 minutes on each side (8 to 10 minutes total cooking time). Sprinkle with a little salt and pepper and serve immediately with one of the recipes from the "Game Sauces" chapter (Lime Marmalade is a good one). Serves 4.

Note: "Excellent."

• • • • •

Fried Chops

> 1½ to 2 pounds chops, about 1 inch thick
> ¼ cup butter or margarine
> ¼ cup dry vermouth or dry white wine
> Salt & pepper

Heat the butter in a heavy skillet over high heat. Add the chops and fry 4 to 5 minutes on each side. Place the cooked chops on a heated platter. Pour the dry vermouth in the hot skillet and scrape the pan with a spatula to remove stuck-on particles. Cook the wine down until there are about 2 tablespoons of liquid. Spoon over chops and serve immediately. Serves 4. A sauce (from the "Game Sauces" chapter) can be offered with the chops.

Note: "Very good."

•   •   •   •   •

Broiled Steak

> 1½ to 2 pounds steak (about 1 inch thick), cut into 4
>   serving pieces
> Soft butter
> ⅛ teaspoon thyme

Spread butter on both sides of the steaks and place on a broiler pan. Sprinkle each steak with a little thyme. Place under a pre-heated broiler, 4 inches from the heat. Broil about 5 minutes on each side (8 to 10 minutes total cooking time). Serve on a heated platter with one of the recipes from the "Game Sauces" chapter (3 M Sauce is great).

Note: "Delicious."

•   •   •   •   •

Buck Valley Steak

> 1½ to 2 pounds steak, cut into 4 1-inch thick serving
>   pieces
> 2 tablespoons butter
> ⅛ teaspoon savory
>   Mushroom Sauce (below)

Heat the butter in a heavy skillet. Fry meat over moderately high heat for 5 minutes on each side. Sprinkle a little savory on the steaks. Remove them to a heated platter. Pour the mushroom sauce into the frying pan and scrape the bottom to loosen meat tidbits and deglaze the pan. Spoon the sauce over the venison steaks and serve immediately. They will be slightly pink on the inside. Serves 4.

Mushroom Sauce:

> 2 tablespoons butter
> 1 cup sliced mushrooms
> ¼ cup port wine
>   Salt & pepper

In a small frying pan, fry mushrooms for 5 minutes in butter. Add port and turn the heat to high. Reduce the liquid by half. Add a little salt and pepper. The sauce is now ready to deglaze the venison steak skillet. Make this sauce before you start frying the steaks.

Note: "Excellent."

• • • • •

Juicy Cheese Steak

> 2 pounds steak, cut into 4 serving pieces
> Flour
> 3 tablespoons cooking oil
> 1 large onion, sliced
> $\frac{1}{4}$ cup chopped green pepper
> 1-pound (16-oz.) can of tomatoes
> $\frac{1}{4}$ teaspoon thyme
> Salt & pepper
> 4 ounces shredded Mozzarella cheese

Dust the steak with flour on both sides. Heat the cooking oil in a heavy skillet and brown the steak on both sides over moderately high heat. Add the onion and green pepper to the pan. Sprinkle the steaks with thyme and a little salt and pepper. Add the tomatoes to the skillet, heat to the boiling point, cover the pan and turn the heat to high simmer. Cook until the meat is fork-tender, about $1\frac{1}{2}$ hours. Sprinkle the cheese equally on top of the steaks, cover the pan and heat until it is well melted, about 5 minutes. Place the steak on a preheated platter and spoon the onion/green pepper/tomato mixture from the pan over the steaks. Serves 4.

Note: "Great recipe."

• • • • •

Les's Swiss Steak

> 4 slices of steak, cut 1 inch thick ($1\frac{1}{2}$ to 2 lbs.)
> $1\frac{1}{2}$ teaspoons dry mustard
> Salt & pepper
> 3 tablespoons butter
> $\frac{2}{3}$ cup beef bouillon
> 1 tablespoon steak sauce
> 2 dashes Tabasco sauce

Using a mallet, pound the dry mustard and a little salt and pepper into both sides of the steak. Brown the meat in a heavy skillet over high heat in the butter. Mix the bouillon, steak sauce, and Tabasco and pour over the steaks. Heat to the boiling point, cover, and reduce the heat to high simmer. Cook until tender, about 1½ hours. Place steaks on a heated platter and spoon the pan juices over them. Garnish with parsley sprigs. Serves 4.

Note: "Very good."

• • • • •

Rolled Steak

> 2 pounds round steak, cut ½ inch thick
> Stuffing (below)
> Flour
> 3 tablespoons margarine
> ½ cup beef bouillon
> ½ cup tomato sauce
> Quick Mixing flour

Make the stuffing and spread it on the steak. Roll the steak up and tie it securely with string. Roll the steak in flour. Heat the margarine in a roasting pan and brown the steak roll on all sides. Mix the bouillon and tomato sauce in a saucepan and heat to the boiling point. Pour over the steak roll, cover and bake in a preheated 350°F. oven for 1½ hours. Place the roll on a heated platter and cut the string. Thicken the pan juices by adding some flour and heating on the stove, stirring until they are slightly thickened. Cut the steak roll into thin slices and ladle the gravy over the pieces. Serves 4 to 6.

Stuffing:

> ¼ cup minced onion
> ¼ cup minced celery
> ¼ cup minced carrots
> ¼ cup margarine
> 2 tablespoons tomato sauce
> 2 cups soft bread crumbs

Fry the vegetables in the margarine in a medium-size skillet until they are tender, about 7 minutes. Add tomato sauce and bread and mix thoroughly.

Note: "Good."

• • • • •

Venison Shish Kebab

> 1½ to 2 pounds venison steak
> 2 sweet green peppers
> 4 onions
> 24 whole mushrooms
> ½ cup dry red wine
> ½ cup cooking oil
> 2 tablespoons soy sauce
> 1 tablespoon dried parsley flakes
> 10 drops Tabasco sauce
> ¼ teaspoon savory
> 1 teaspoon celery seed
> ¼ teaspoon pepper

Trim all fat and sinew from the meat and cut into bite-size pieces. Quarter the onions. Cut the green peppers into chunks. Using four large skewers, alternately thread the meat chunks on with pieces of pepper and onion and mushrooms. (Other vegetables such as tomato and celery chunks can be substituted.) Mix the wine, cooking oil, soy sauce, parsley, Tabasco, savory, celery seed, and pepper together. Place the skewers on a large, flat dish or pan with up-turned edges (such as a cookie sheet) and pour the marinade over the laden skewers. Refrigerate for 2 to 3 hours, turning the skewers every 30 minutes. Place a piece of foil on a broiler pan. Preheat the broiler. Put the skewers on the foil and broil for 6 minutes on each side, about 4 inches from the heat (total cooking time is about 12 minutes). Baste with marinade once during the cooking. Serves 4.

Note: "Very good."

•　•　•　•　•

STEW MEAT

Hunters often have all of their extra meat (after roasts, chops, and steaks are cut) ground into burger. However, it's fun to save some of it for hearty stews. Nothing tastes much better on a cold winter evening. Tough shoulder and lower leg meat make tasty stews, and long cooking recipes tenderize them beautifully.

Recipe Notes:

Carter Camp Stew—preparation time, about 40 minutes—rich and hearty.

Game Barley Stew—preparation time, about 30 minutes—sturdy and different.

Rountree Stew—preparation time, about 25 minutes—simple and delicious.

Nine Mile Stew—preparation time, about 35 minutes—old-fashioned stew flavor.

Carter Camp Stew

> 1 pound stew meat
> 3 slices bacon, chopped
> Flour seasoned with salt & pepper
> 1 garlic clove, minced
> 2 cups water
> 1 beef bouillon cube
> ½ cup tomato juice
> ¼ cup port wine
> 1 teaspoon lemon juice
> 1 teaspoon steak sauce
> ½ teaspoon thyme
> 4 small onions
> 4 carrots, cut into pieces
> 4 potatoes, quartered
> 1 cup chopped celery
> Salt & pepper
> Quick Mixing flour

Brown bacon in a Dutch oven over medium-high heat. Roll stew meat in flour mixture. Brown the meat on all sides. Add garlic and cook for 1 minute. Add water, bouillon cube, tomato juice, port, lemon juice, steak sauce, and thyme. Cover and cook over low heat for about 1 hour, until the meat starts to get tender. Watch liquid and add more water, if necessary. Add onions, carrots, potatoes, and celery to the Dutch oven, cover, and simmer another hour, or until all is tender. Add salt and pepper to taste. Thicken the stew a little by sprinkling with a little flour, stirring until it is well mixed and thick. Serves 4.

Note: "Very good."

• • • • •

Game Barley Stew

1 pound stew meat, cut into chunks
Flour
2 tablespoons cooking oil
$2\frac{1}{2}$ cups water
1 cup canned tomatoes, cut into small pieces
1 onion, sliced
$\frac{1}{2}$ teaspoon salt
Pepper
1 cup sliced carrots
$\frac{1}{2}$ cup sliced celery
$\frac{1}{3}$ cup finely chopped green pepper
$\frac{1}{3}$ cup quick cooking barley
2 tablespoons chopped parsley
1 dash Tabasco sauce
Quick Mixing flour (optional)

In a Dutch oven or large skillet, heat the oil. Roll the meat in flour and brown over medium-high heat. Add water, tomatoes, onion, salt, and a little pepper to the pot and cover. Simmer for $1\frac{1}{2}$ hours, until the meat is almost tender. Add the carrots, celery, green pepper, barley, parsley, and Tabasco. Mix well, cover, and simmer another 45 minutes. If you wish, thicken the stew a bit by sprinkling with a little flour while stirring. Serves 4.

Note: "Delicious."

•　•　•　•　•

Rountree Stew

> 1 to 1½ pounds stew meat, cut into chunks.
> Flour
> 3 tablespoons margarine
> Salt & pepper
> 1 large onion
> 1 large can tomatoes (1 lb., 12 oz.)
> ¼ teaspoon marjoram
> 4 potatoes, peeled and quartered
> 4 carrots, peeled and quartered
> Quick Mixing flour

Roll the pieces of stew meat in flour and brown in a Dutch oven or a large, heavy skillet in hot margarine over medium-high heat. Sprinkle with a little salt and pepper. Add onion, tomatoes, and marjoram to the pot; cut the tomatoes into small pieces. Cover and heat to the boiling point. Turn the heat to simmer and cook until the meat starts to tenderize, about 1 hour. Add potatoes and carrots and cook until tender, about 45 minutes to 1 hour. Thicken the stew by sprinkling with flour while stirring. Serves 4 to 6.

Note: "Good."

• • • • •

Nine Mile Stew

> 1 to 1½ pounds stew meat, cut into chunks
> 2 tablespoons cooking oil
> 2 cups hot water
> 2 teaspoons steak sauce
> 1 garlic clove, minced
> 1 large onion, sliced
> 1 bay leaf
> ½ teaspoon salt
> Pepper
> 1 green pepper, cut into chunks
> 4 carrots, quartered
> 4 potatoes, quartered
> Quick Mixing flour

Heat the oil in a Dutch oven and brown the meat over medium-high heat. Add the water, steak sauce, garlic, onion, bay leaf, salt, and a little pepper to the pot. Cover and simmer for about 1 hour, until the meat starts to tenderize. Add green pepper, carrots, and potatoes to the pot, cover, and simmer for another 45 minutes to 1 hour. Correct salt and pepper if necessary. Thicken with flour. Serves 4 to 6.

Note: "Very good."

• • • • •

GROUND MEAT

Meat from the front and lower back legs, ribs, and at times, the shoulder, is often ground into burger. Before grinding, all the natural fat should be removed because it is usually a bit strong in flavor and spoils easily. However, the best ground meat has either beef suet or fatty pork mixed in while it is being ground; juicy meat is the result. A ratio of $\frac{1}{4}$ pound of suet or $\frac{1}{3}$ pound of pork is about right for each pound of wild meat. If pork is used, the ground meat must always be well cooked.

Basically, ground wild meat can be used in any recipe structured for domestic burger. However, it's fun to have a few special dishes. I've included my favorites in this section.

To enjoy the pure flavor, broiled burgers should be the first ground-meat meal tasted from a big-game animal. Count on four fat patties per pound. Place the patties on a broiler pan, salt and pepper lightly, and place under a preheated broiler, about four inches from the heat. Cook for about five minutes on each side for medium rare (an extra 5 to 7 minutes for well done) and serve on heated hamburger buns.

Recipe Notes:

Minnesota Wild Rice Casserole—preparation time, about 35 minutes—delicious, hearty, one-dish meal.

Robinson Chili—preparation time, about 30 minutes—hot and spicy.

Mother's Meatballs—preparation time, about 40 minutes—great, pungent flavor.

Hunter's Oven Dinner—preparation time, about 1 hour—hearty winter dinner.

Grabe Meat Loaf—preparation time, about 20 minutes—juicy and filling.

Minnesota Wild Rice Casserole

    1 cup uncooked wild rice
    2 tablespoons butter
    1 cup chopped onion
    1 cup chopped celery
    1 pound ground meat
    Salt & pepper
    1 can cream of mushroom soup
    1 soup can of water
    3 1-ounce slices of American cheese

Wash wild rice in cold water and drain. Put the rice in a large saucepan with plenty of hot water. Bring to a boil. Cook over moderate heat for 35 minutes, until the hulls are tender and swollen. Drain the rice. Heat the butter in a large skillet. Fry the onion and celery over medium-high heat for 5 to 7 minutes. Add ground meat and brown. Sprinkle with a little salt and pepper. Add soup, water, and drained rice. Mix well and turn into a large, buttered casserole. Break the cheese into small pieces and stick into the rice mixture. Place the casserole, uncovered in a preheated 350°F. oven for 40 minutes. Serve with a green salad and hot rolls. Serves 4 to 6.

Note: "Very good."

• • • • •

Robinson Chili

- 2½ pounds ground meat
- 2 large onions, finely chopped
- 1 garlic clove, minced
- 3 tablespoons cooking oil
- 1 tablespoon steak sauce
- 1 teaspoon salt
- 2 packages prepared chili mix
- 1 to 2 tablespoons chili powder (depends on how hot you like it)
- 18 ounces tomato juice, or more
- 1 tablespoon basil
- ½ teaspoon oregano
- 2 cups applesauce
- 2 15-ounce cans pinto beans

Brown the meat, onions, and garlic in hot oil in a Dutch oven. Add the steak sauce, salt, chili mix, chili powder, tomato juice, basil, and oregano and mix well. Bring the mixture to the boiling point, lower heat to simmer, cover and cook for two hours, stirring occasionally. Add a little tomato juice if it gets too thick and starts to stick to the bottom of the pot. Add applesauce and beans, mix, and cook another hour uncovered. Chili should be very thick. (Don't let the applesauce fool you; the dish is not one bit sweet.) Serves 6. Leftovers make great Sloppy Joe material, serve on hamburger rolls.

Note: "Hot and delicious."

•　•　•　•　•

Mother's Meatballs

            1 pound ground meat
            2 tablespoons finely chopped onions
            2 tablespoons finely chopped green pepper
            1 beaten egg
            ½ cup milk
            ⅓ cup cornmeal
            ½ teaspoon salt
            1½ teaspoons dry mustard
            1 teaspoon chili powder
              Flour
            ¼ cup cooking oil
              Spaghetti sauce

Combine meat, onions, green pepper, egg, milk, cornmeal, salt, dry mustard, and chili powder in a large bowl, mixing thoroughly. Form into 12 to 14 meatballs and roll them in flour. Heat the oil in a large skillet and brown the balls, a few at a time. Pour your favorite spaghetti sauce into the skillet, cover, and simmer for 30 to 40 minutes. Serve with hot spaghetti. Serves 4 to 6.

Note: "Best meatballs I've ever tasted."

• • • • •

Hunter's Oven Dinner

            1 recipe of Mother's Meatballs (previous recipe)
            4 to 6 medium-size onions
            4 to 6 medium-size potatoes, peeled and quartered
            4 to 6 carrots, peeled and quartered
            1 large can tomato juice (1 qt., 14 oz.)

Make the meatball recipe according to instructions. Place the browned meatballs in a roasting pan. Add the onions, potatoes, and carrots to the pan. Pour half of the tomato juice in the skillet that was used to brown the meatballs. Heat until it is boiling, scraping the bottom of the pan to remove the tidbits of meat. Pour over the vegetables and meatballs in the roasting pan. Add enough more hot tomato juice to cover the vegetables. Cover the roasting pan and place in a preheated 350°F. oven for at least 2 hours, until the vegetables are tender. Serves 4 to 6.

Note: "Excellent."

•   •   •   •   •

Grabe Meat Loaf

> 1½ pounds ground meat
> 1 beaten egg
> 1 medium-size onion, chopped
> 1 can vegetable soup (10¾ oz.)
> 1 small can tomato sauce (8 oz.)
>   Salt & pepper
> 3 cups Rice Krispies cereal

In a large bowl mix meat, egg, onion, soup, and half of the can of tomato sauce. Sprinkle with a little salt and pepper and add the Rice Krispies. Mix thoroughly. Form into a large oblong ball and place in a roasting pan. Pour the rest of the tomato sauce over the meat loaf, cover and put in a preheated 350°F. oven for 1½ hours. Slice and serve. Serves 6 to 8.

Note: "Excellent."

•   •   •   •   •

HEART & LIVER

What a shame to see the heart and liver discarded by hunters when they clean a big-game animal. The organs are rich in vitamins and full of flavor plus being free of the quick-growth hormones that settle in the liver of most domestically grown animals. Try my recipes and you'll agree that the organs are too valuable to discard.

Recipe Notes:

Pickled Heart—preparation time, about 20 minutes—hearty sandwich material.

Fried Liver—preparation time, about 20 minutes—tender meat, filling dish.

Louisiana Game Liver—preparation time, about 35 minutes—Creole-type dish.

Curried Heart Toast Rounds—preparation time, about 30 minutes—spicy and rich.

Liver Appetizers—preparation time, about 35 minutes—creamy and filling.

Pickled Heart

> 1 well-cleaned heart
> 2 bay leaves
>   Salt & pepper
> 1 onion sliced
> $\frac{1}{3}$ cup wine vinegar
> $\frac{2}{3}$ cup cold water

Place the heart in a pot of water with the bay leaves and enough water to cover the heart. Bring the water to a boil, reduce heat, and cover the pot. Cook until the heart is fork-tender, the time depends on the age of the animal; count on at least two hours. Cool and cut the heart into thin slices, removing any valve tissue. Place the slices in a nonmetal bowl with the onion. Add some salt and pepper. Cover with vinegar and water, adding more if necessary. Cover and refrigerate for 12 hours. Before using, pat dry with paper towels. The heart may be eaten as finger food or used in sandwiches.

Note: "Great."

• • • • •

Fried Liver

>   1 pound liver
>   Flour
>   2 tablespoons butter
>   2 tablespoons cooking oil
>   Salt & pepper
>   1 onion, sliced

Cut the liver with a very sharp knife, into *thin* slices. It's easier to slice if the liver is semifrozen before cutting. Dredge the liver in flour. Heat the butter and oil in a large skillet and cook the onion for about 7 minutes, until tender. Remove the onions and reserve. Have a platter, covered with paper towels in a 150° F. oven. Fry the liver, a few slices at a time, for about 4 minutes on a side. The time depends on how thin the slices are but the liver should be removed from the pan while the juices are still running red. It will continue to cook for a minute while it is being kept warm. The result should be a well-browned exterior while the interior is still a bit pink. *Overcooking results in tough liver.* As each piece is removed to the heated platter, add more to the pan until all is cooked. Add more butter and oil as necessary. When all the liver has been cooked, return the onions to the pan and reheat. Serve liver and onions on a heated platter. Serves 4. Add a little salt and pepper.

Note: "Excellent."

• • • • •

Louisiana Game Liver

>   1 pound liver
>   Flour
>   3 tablespoons margarine
>   1 onion, chopped
>   1 rib celery, chopped
>   1 green pepper, chopped
>   1 16-ounce can of tomatoes
>   4 drops Tabasco sauce (or more)
>   Salt & pepper

Slice liver into strips, about ½-inch-by-2-inches. Dust the strips lightly with flour. Heat the margarine in a large skillet over medium-high heat and brown the strips on all sides, about 5 minutes cooking time. Don't crowd the pan; fry in batches, adding more margarine if necessary. Remove the liver from the pan and set aside. Add the onion, celery, and green pepper to the skillet and cook for about 3 minutes, stirring. Add the tomatoes and Tabasco. More Tabasco can be added if you like your dishes hot. Cut the tomatoes into manageable small pieces. Bring to a boil, cover, turn the heat to simmer, and cook for 12 to 15 minutes. Sprinkle with a little salt and pepper and thicken the sauce with Quick Mixing flour. Stir while sprinkling with just enough flour to slightly thicken. Add liver strips to the pan and simmer for another 2 minutes. Don't overcook or the liver will be tough. Serve on hot cooked long grain rice. Serves 4.

Note: "Very good."

• • • • •

Curried Heart Toast Rounds

1 cup finely chopped, cooked heart
4 tablespoons butter or margarine
1 teaspoon curry powder
3 tablespoons flour
1 cup milk
2 tablespoons chili sauce
Parmesan cheese
Melba toast rounds

Cook the heart in enough water to cover until it is tender. Cut into small pieces and put it through a meat grinder or chop in a good blender or food processor. Melt the butter in a skillet and mix in the flour and curry powder. Slowly add the milk, stirring over moderate heat until the mixture thickens. Blend in the heart and chili sauce. Spread the mixture on toast rounds, sprinkle with a little Parmesan cheese and place on a baking sheet.

Bake in a preheated 375°F. oven for 5 to 7 minutes. Serve hot as an appetizer.

Note: "Delicious."

• • • • •

Liver Appetizers

    1 pound liver
    2 tablespoons minced green onion
    3 tablespoons butter
    3 tablespoons flour
      Salt & pepper
    1 cup light cream
      Dash of Tabasco sauce
    1 teaspoon lemon juice
    2 egg yolks, slightly beaten
    ½ cup grated Swiss cheese
      Cocktail pumpernickel bread

Cut the liver into very thin pieces. In a frying pan, cook onion and liver in butter until tender, about 7 minutes. Put in a blender in small batches (or use a food processor) and chop into fine bits. Return to frying pan. Blend in flour and a little salt and pepper. Add cream slowly, stirring over low heat until the mixture is thick. Blend in Tabasco and lemon juice. Add a small amount of the hot mixture to the egg yolks. Stir and return the mixture to the frying pan. Heat and stir constantly for 2 minutes. Spread the mixture on bread rounds and place on a baking sheet. Top with cheese and bake in a 350°F. oven for 15 minutes. Serve immediately.

Note: "Very good."

• • • • •

LEFTOVERS

A good-size roast often leaves plenty of cooked meat and gravy for another dinner dish as well as sandwiches. For top flavor, refrigerate the meat immediately after the meal, covered completely with a good quality plastic wrap (I use Reynolds). Utilize the meat within two or three days. If kept longer, the leftovers should be frozen. Double wrap with plastic and freezer paper and use within two or three weeks for best results.

Recipe Notes:

Coles Creek Venison—cubed, cooked meat—preparation time, about 30 minutes—rich, filling dish.

Meat Pie—cubed, cooked meat—preparation time, about 35 minutes—delicious, old-fashioned meat pie flavor.

Sandwich Spread—ground, cooked meat—preparation time, about 25 minutes—juicy, rich spread.

Sloppy Joe—finely chopped, cooked meat—preparation time, about 10 minutes, robust sandwich.

Coles Creek Venison

      3 cups diced, cooked meat
      1 cup Orzo (rice-shaped pasta—long grain rice may be
          substituted)
      ½ cup chopped onions
      ¼ cup chopped green pepper
      2 cups sliced mushrooms
      6 tablespoons butter or margarine
      ½ cup red wine
      ¼ cup leftover gravy (or a little more)
      1 teaspoon savory
      1 tablespoon chopped parsley

Cook Orzo according to directions and rinse under hot water. Drain well and reserve. In a large skillet, fry onions, green pepper, and mushrooms over medium-high heat in the butter until tender, about 7 minutes. Add the meat and brown. Add the wine, gravy, savory, and cooked Orzo to the skillet and mix well. Stir until thoroughly hot, adding more gravy if you wish. Sprinkle with parsley and serve with a green salad and hot rolls. Serves 4 to 6.

Note: "Delicious."

• • • • •

Meat Pie

>   2 to 3 cups leftover roast, cut into bite-size chunks
>   1 small onion, chopped
>   1 rib of celery, chopped
>   2 carrots, sliced
>   1 large potato, diced
> $\frac{1}{2}$ cup leftover gravy
> $\frac{1}{4}$ teaspoon marjoram
>   Salt & pepper
>   Quick Mixing flour
>   Pie crust (optional)

Place the onion, celery, carrots, and potato in a saucepan with just enough water to cover. Cook until all are done, about 20 minutes. Add the gravy, marjoram, a little salt and pepper, and mix well. Sprinkle the mixture with enough Quick Mixing flour, while stirring, to thicken the liquid. Add the meat, heat, and mix. Turn the mixture into a buttered, oven-proof casserole that is just large enough to hold it. Top the meat pie with your favorite crust if you wish. If you don't use a pie crust, cover the casserole with its lid or aluminum foil. Place the pie crust laden dish in a preheated 425°F. oven and bake for 15 minutes, until the crust starts to brown. Lower the heat to 350°F. and cook another 15 minutes or until it starts to bubble. Without the crust, bake at 350°F. for about 35 minutes. Serve with hot biscuits or rolls and a green salad. Serves 4.

Note: "Yummy."

• • • • •

Sandwich Spread

> 1 pound ground, cooked meat
> ½ cup chili sauce
> ¾ cup mayonnaise (or more)
> 1 tablespoon horseradish
> Salt & pepper to taste

Grind leftover roast meat with the coarse head on an electric or hand grinder. Add rest of ingredients and mix well. More mayonnaise may be added if a juicier spread is desired. Check salt and pepper by tasting, adding more if necessary. Serve as sandwich spread on bread or as an appetizer with crackers.

Note: "Great."

•　•　•　•　•

Sloppy Joe

> Finely chopped leftover meat
> Butter
> Catsup
> Tabasco
> Hamburger rolls

Chop leftover meat into small pieces and put in a skillet with some butter. The amount depends on how many sandwiches you wish to make. For one fat sandwich, use ⅓ cup meat and 1 tablespoon of butter. Mix the meat and butter and heat over moderate temperature. Add enough catsup to make a juicy sandwich. Spice it up with a dash of Tabasco, heat well, and serve on a heated hamburger roll.

Note: "Very good."

•　•　•　•　•

APPETIZERS

Roast leftovers, ground meat, and liver can be used to prepare some great appetizers. It's a kick at a party to watch those who have always protested that they don't like game devour delicious tidbits made from big-game animals. They change their tone quickly. My favorite recipes are included in this chapter. Try them and enjoy.

Recipe Notes:

Cocktail Meatballs—ground meat—preparation time, about 25 minutes—spicy taste.

Liver Pâté—liver—preparation time, about 25 minutes—rich flavor.

Rye Tasties—leftover roast meat—preparation time, about 15 minutes—robust.

Stuffed Mushrooms—ground meat—preparation time, about 30 minutes—hearty appetizer.

Creamy Game Ball—leftover roast meat—preparation time, about 20 minutes—mild flavor.

Savory Game Dip—ground meat—preparation time, about 20 minutes—light, creamy flavor.

Cocktail Meatballs

$1\frac{1}{2}$ pounds ground meat
2 eggs, beaten
$\frac{1}{4}$ cup minced onion
$\frac{1}{8}$ teaspoon garlic powder
3 tablespoons chopped parsley
$\frac{1}{4}$ teaspoon paprika
1 teaspoon lemon juice
3 tablespoons Parmesan cheese
$\frac{1}{4}$ teaspoon oregano
2 tablespoons butter
1 8-ounce can tomato sauce

Mix ground meat, eggs, onion, garlic powder, parsley, paprika, lemon juice, cheese, and oregano together thoroughly. Form the mixture into tiny balls. Heat butter in a large, heavy skillet and brown the meatballs on all sides in the skillet. Pour the tomato sauce over the meatballs, cover, turn the heat to low, and simmer for 30 minutes. Serve warm with toothpicks.

Note: "Absolutely delicious."

• • • • •

Liver Pâté

$\frac{1}{2}$ pound venison liver, finely chopped
2 tablespoons butter
$\frac{1}{4}$ cup finely chopped onion
$\frac{1}{4}$ cup finely chopped mushrooms
2 tablespoons white wine
2 tablespoons whipping cream (or more)
1 tablespoon brandy
1 egg, hard cooked and finely chopped
2 tablespoons minced parsley
Salt & pepper to taste

Heat butter in a skillet and fry onion and mushrooms over moderate heat until limp, about 5 minutes. Transfer with a slotted spoon to a good blender or food processor. Add the liver to the skillet and fry for 3 minutes, stirring constantly. Add the wine to the skillet and scrape the bottom with a spatula. Pour the liver and pan juices into the blender. Add the cream and brandy. Blend well, adding a little more cream, if necessary, to make a spreadable consistency. Transfer from blender to a bowl and blend in the egg and parsley. Add a little salt and pepper and serve with crackers. Can be served warm or cold. (If the pâté is a little thin, chill before serving.)

Note: "Great."

• • • • •

Rye Tasties

> 1 cup minced, cooked, leftover meat
> $\frac{1}{2}$ cup mayonnaise
> $\frac{1}{3}$ cup chopped onion
>   Dash of steak sauce
>   Salt & pepper to taste
>   Parmesan cheese

Cut the meat into fine pieces or use a food processor. Mix the meat, mayonnaise, chopped onion, steak sauce, and a little salt and pepper together well and refrigerate for several hours to marry the flavors. Spread the mixture on small rye bread rounds and sprinkle with cheese. Broil about 4 inches from the heat until bubbly and brown. Cool slightly and serve.

Note: "Excellent."

•   •   •   •   •

Stuffed Mushrooms

> 24 large mushrooms
> $\frac{1}{4}$ pound ground meat
> 2 tablespoons butter
> $\frac{1}{4}$ cup finely chopped green pepper
> $\frac{1}{4}$ cup finely chopped onion
> $\frac{1}{2}$ cup soft bread crumbs
> 2 tablespoons chopped parsley
>   White wine or dry vermouth

Clean mushrooms and remove stems. (Most mushrooms need only to be wiped with a paper towel and not washed.) Melt butter in a skillet. Chop the mushroom stems and put in skillet with the meat, green pepper, and onion. Fry until the vegetables are limp and the meat brown. Drain off the fat. Add bread, parsley, and enough wine to moisten. Stuff the mushroom caps. Place in a shallow baking dish with a small amount of water (about $\frac{1}{4}$-inch deep). Bake in a preheated 350°F. oven for 20 minutes. Serve warm.

Note: "Great."

· · · · ·

Creamy Game Ball

    1 cup minced, cooked meat
    2 tablespoons finely chopped green olives
    1 tablespoon prepared mustard
    2 tablespoons soft butter
    3 ounces softened cream cheese
    2 tablespoons finely chopped parsley

Grind the meat or finely mince it. Blend it with the olives, mustard, butter, and cheese until thoroughly mixed. Form into a ball and roll in parsley. Chill for one hour until serving time. Serve with crackers.

Note: "Very good."

· · · · ·

Savory Game Dip

    $\frac{1}{2}$ pound ground meat
    1 small onion, minced
    2 tablespoons butter or margarine
    8 ounces cream cheese
    1 teaspoon steak sauce
    $\frac{1}{2}$ teaspoon thyme
    Milk, about 4 tablespoons
    Salt & pepper to taste
    Paprika
    Parsley sprigs

Break the meat into tiny pieces. Cook it and the onion in butter over low heat until it is brown. Drain the meat thoroughly on paper towels and cool. Let cheese soften to room temperature. Mix cheese, meat/onion, steak sauce, and thyme well. Mix in enough milk to make a good dip consistency. Add salt and pepper to taste. Sprinkle with paprika. Serve with potato chips, vegetable, or bread sticks. If the dip is chilled before serving, bring it back to room temperature. Add a little milk if necessary.

Note: "Good."

•　•　•　•　•

Trapped Game

The trapping of animals and the resulting barter or sale of their skin and fur has been an active occupation all through man's history. As with many other endeavors, trapping wild animals is a lot more difficult than someone who has never done it might suspect. A successful trapper must be a keen observer of nature since knowing the habits and likely environment of the animal is essential. While watching a demonstration on how to lay a trap for a fox, I found it was involved and time consuming with dozens of details that had to be just right before the fox could be lured into it.

Modern day trappers are under strict regulations, many of them imposed by wildlife agencies after being requested by the trappers themselves. Like all responsible hunters, trappers wish to perpetuate the animals they love to pursue. There are regulations dealing with types of traps, how often they must be visited, how many animals may be taken and a multitude of other rules. There is perhaps more emotional hysteria involved in the antitrapping segment of our population than toward any other aspect of hunting. Mostly, this is due to the encroachment of human population on rural areas, the traditional stomping grounds of trappers. Pets that are allowed to roam free sometimes go to the wrong place at the wrong time.

Early settlers valued trapped animals for their meat as well as their skin. Even the fat was coveted by trappers who craved it because their diets were low in fats, vegetables, and sugar. Until recently I had not cooked many of the traditionally trapped game. Then a trapper friend supplied me with well-cleaned raccoon, muskrat, and fox and I set about learning more about cooking them. The first thing I discovered is that there hasn't been much written by trustworthy game cooks about these animals. So, I followed my instincts in experimenting with them. If I haven't covered an animal you wish to cook, do the same thing. Try different approaches until you find a combination you like.

The first priority for good tasting meat is a well-dressed animal. Because the fat is often strong, it should be removed. Naturally, young animals will be more tender than old ones. Parboil the older meat to tenderize it before proceeding with a recipe. You can expect the meat from carnivorous animals such as fox to be slightly sweet. As far as answering the question of how raccoon, muskrat, or fox taste, the answer is: they taste like themselves, just as pork tastes only like pork and beef tastes like beef.

With most of the fur bearers I've tried, Zinfandel, my all-American favorite, seems to work beautifully. Zinfandel has been mentioned several times in this cookbook, but it's a great choice for so many entrees that come from the wild. But don't make the mistake of believing that all Zinfandels taste exactly the same. It's just like French Bordeaux. Some of them are full of character, some are not and there are dozens in the middle ground of taste sensations. Generally, Zinfandel is a semidry wine, not very sweet, with a decided aroma of berries and herbs about it. In some Zinfandels the sweetness may be a bit pronounced or they may be quite dry—it depends on how the wine was made and when.

With "Roast Raccoon," a jug of Inglenook Navelle Zinfandel was opened and it was a perfect complement. Gallo Zinfandel was tried with the fox dish and while it wasn't as dry, it too blended nicely with the slightly sweet meat.

California Burgundy and most of the Italian reds are also excellent choices for the "odd" animals, in case you don't like the berrylike aftertaste of Zinfandel.

Tip: To bring the flavor of jug wine to its fullest, pour out half of the contents into a decanter or another wine bottle 20 minutes before serving. The exposure to air will "round out" the taste and it will be much more pleasant than it would be straight from the bottle.

Recipe Notes:

Roast Raccoon—serving pieces—preparation time, about 30 minutes—rich, robust meal.

Fried Raccoon—serving pieces; good recipe for older animal—preparation time, about 25 minutes—mild-flavored meat.

Charcoal Grilled Raccoon—young animal, cut in serving pieces—preparation time, about 10 minutes—spicy, fruity taste.

Muskrat Jambalaya—whole animal—preparation time, about 30 minutes—hot and spicy.

Roast Fox—hind quarters—preparation time, about 10 minutes—rich, filling dish.

Fox Stew—chunks of meat—preparation time, about 25 minutes—slightly sweet, full-bodied stew.

Roast Raccoon

> 1 raccoon, cut into serving pieces
> Flour
> 3 tablespoons cooking oil
> 4 small onions
> 1 beef bouillon cube
> 1 cup water
> 1 tablespoon steak sauce
> 4 to 6 medium-size potatoes, cut into large chunks
> 4 to 6 carrots, cut into large chunks
> Salt & pepper

Roll the raccoon pieces in the flour. In a frying pan, heat the oil and brown the raccoon pieces on all sides in the hot oil. Place the pieces in a roasting pan with the onion, bouillon cube (crush it with the back of a spoon), water, and steak sauce. Cover the pan and roast in a preheated 350°F. oven until the meat starts to tenderize (you can penetrate it with a meat fork). This will take from 45 minutes to 1½ hours, depending on the age of the animal. Add the potatoes and carrots, sprinkle them with a little salt and pepper (you can add more at the table if necessary), cover the pan and roast until everything is done—about 1 hour. Thicken the sauce by placing 2 tablespoons of flour in a jar with ⅓ cup of water, shake well and add to the pan liquids. Stir constantly while heating the pan juices and remove from the heat when they are thick. Serve with the meat and vegetables. The pan juices may be served as is with the dish; they will be just as good, just thinner. Serves 4 to 6 depending on the size of the raccoon. Serving Suggestion: for 4 servings, add 4 potatoes and carrots; when serving 6 people, cook 6 of each.

Note: "Very good."

• • • • •

Fried Raccoon

        1 raccoon, cut into serving pieces
        1 bay leaf
        1 chicken bouillon cube
          Water to cover the meat
        1 beaten egg
          Flavored bread crumbs (available in the bread section
            of supermarkets)
        3 tablespoons cooking oil

Place the raccoon pieces in a large pot with the bay leaf, bouillon cube, and enough water to cover the meat. Cover the pot and cook over high simmer until it is tender (when a fork is easily inserted in the meat). Remove the meat from the broth with a slotted spoon, dry on paper towels, dip in the egg and roll in the bread crumbs. Heat the oil in a large frying pan. Brown the raccoon pieces on all sides in the hot oil and serve immediately. Serves 4 to 6.

Tip: I buy flavored bread crumbs; however you can make your own by drying slices of bread in a 250°F. oven until all the moisture is gone, then use a rolling pin to crush them and add a little garlic powder, onion powder, and parsley flakes to them.

Note: "Good."

•   •   •   •   •

Charcoal Grilled Raccoon

> 1 raccoon, cut into serving pieces (young animal)
> $\frac{1}{2}$ cup white wine
> 2 tablespoons soy sauce
> 2 tablespoons orange marmalade
> $\frac{1}{2}$ cup catsup
> $\frac{1}{8}$ teaspoon garlic powder

Mix a marinade by combining the wine, soy sauce, marmalade, catsup, and garlic powder thoroughly. Place the marinade in a shallow glass container, large enough to hold the raccoon in a single layer. Roll the pieces of meat in the marinade, cover, and refrigerate overnight or about 12 hours. Turn the meat over a couple of times during the marinating period. Cook over medium-hot charcoal until it is tender, turning and basting with the marinade several times. A young animal will probably take about 30 minutes (don't use this recipe for an older animal). The time depends on the weather and the heat of the coals. Serves 4 to 6.

Note: "Very good."

•   •   •   •   •

Muskrat Jambalaya

    1 muskrat, skinned and cleaned
    1 onion slice
    1 bay leaf
    1 beef bouillon cube
    2 tablespoons butter
    2 tablespoons flour
    1 onion, chopped
    1 garlic clove, minced
    2 green onions, chopped
    $\frac{1}{4}$ cup chopped green pepper
    1 tablespoon minced parsley
    1 cup chopped tomatoes with juice
    2 cups broth (from cooking muskrat)
    2 pinches ground cloves
    2 pinches ground allspice
    1 pinch red pepper (or more)
    $\frac{1}{4}$ teaspoon thyme
    $\frac{1}{2}$ teaspoon salt
    Pepper to taste
    1 cup uncooked long grain rice

Cook muskrat in water to cover with the onion slice, bay leaf, and bouillon cube until the meat is very tender, from 1 to 1$\frac{1}{2}$ hours. Strip meat from the bones and cut into bite-size pieces. Save broth.

Melt butter over a low heat in a heavy saucepan. Stir in flour and cook until it's golden, about 5 minutes. Add onions, garlic, green pepper, and parsley. Turn heat to medium, stir, and cook for 10 minutes. Add tomatoes, 2 cups of the broth from cooking the muskrat, cloves, allspice, thyme, salt, and pepper. Add red pepper to taste. Mix in rice and muskrat pieces. Stir well, bring to a boil, then lower heat to simmer, cover, and cook for 20 minutes until the rice is done but the mixture is still damp. Serve with a green salad. Serves 4. (The meat can be cooked ahead of time and stored in the refrigerator.)

Note: "Great recipe."

• • • • •

Roast Fox

Hind quarters of a 7-pound dressed fox
1 can golden mushroom soup
1 pkg. dried onion soup mix
$\frac{1}{3}$ cup beer

Place the meat in a large piece of heavy-duty aluminum foil. Mix the soups and beer and pour over meat. Seal package and place in a roasting pan. Roast in a preheated 350°F. oven for $2\frac{1}{2}$ to 3 hours, until the meat is fork tender. Halfway through the roasting period, open the package and turn the meat over in the sauce. Reseal the foil package and return to the oven. Serve the sauce in a gravy boat to be ladled over the meat at the table. Serves 4.

Note: "Rich and good."

• • • • •

Fox Stew

$1\frac{1}{2}$ pounds of meat, cut into bite-size chunks
$\frac{1}{4}$ cup flour
2 tablespoons butter
1 medium onion, sliced
1 tablespoon chopped parsley
1 cup whole mushrooms
1 bay leaf
Salt (about $\frac{1}{2}$ teaspoon)
Pepper
$\frac{1}{2}$ cup Burgundy wine
$\frac{1}{2}$ cup water
Parsley sprigs

Place meat in a paper or plastic bag with flour and shake to coat the meat thoroughly. Heat the butter in a large skillet. Add meat and brown it on all sides over medium-high heat. When all sides are brown, add onion, parsley, mushrooms, bay leaf, salt, pepper, wine, and water. Stir, cover, and reduce heat (once the liquid is boiling) to simmer. Cook from 1 to 1½ hours, until the meat is tender. Serve, ladled over hot, buttered rice. Garnish with parsley. Serves 4.

Note: "Good."

•   •   •   •   •

Smoking Game

Raves will come your way when you serve smoked game. Best of all, it is easy to do. Smoking wild game has become very popular recently because commercial home smokers are readily available in sporting goods stores and outdoor mail-order catalogs. These various smokers are fueled by electricity, charcoal, or propane.

Our forefathers would not have recognized the smoking process we use today. They smoked to preserve meat because they had limited refrigeration. It involved a salty brine, a large home-made smokehouse and many days (even weeks) of constantly tending the very low, smoky fire. The finished product was dried but not cooked. The moisture was removed.

Our smoking these days should really be called smoke cooking since the meat is slowly cooked over low heat while it is being permeated with a delicious smoky flavor from hardwood chips or sawdust. While the game will keep up to two weeks under refrigeration, it is not really a preservation method because it must be chilled. Since the meat does not have to be brined in a heavy salt mixture to preserve it, smoke-cooked game is more pleasant to eat than the salty meats from old-time smoking methods.

There are two basic types of commercial smokers on the

market. One is the dry-heat model like the Little Chief, Outers, and Mirro. The other is the moist-heat model such as the Brinkman Smoke 'N Pit and the Coleman Smoke Cooker. The moisture is supplied by a water pan which sets beneath the heat source and the meat. The dry-heat units use electric heat. The moist-heat types can be electric, charcoal, or propane. An advantage of the moist-heat smoker is that it can also be used as a summer backyard barbecue or charcoal grill.

Game smoked in the dry-heat models tends to reduce in moisture content which makes the meat more suitable for snacking and appetizers since the meat is intense and rich. Moist-heat smoked food is often used for the main course in dinners. The meat is juicy with a lightly smoked flavor.

Hardwood chips and sawdust provide the smoky flavor. Hickory, apple, cherry, and maple are the most commonly used species. Softwoods and conifers should be avoided since they impart a bitter taste. Guidelines on how many pans of sawdust or how many chips to add to the smoker are just that. Add more for an intense smoky flavor, less for a more delicate taste. Sawdust for electric dry-heat smokers can be purchased from the same dealer that supplied your smoker. When the wood chips that come with a moist-heat model are gone, it is easy to cut your own while pruning tree limbs. If the wood chips are dry, soak them in water for a half hour before using. This helps produce more smoke. Green wood chips do not need soaking; they'll burn slowly and produce a lot of smoke without it.

The timing of smoked game is an inexact science, especially if charcoal is used. The size of the game, the air temperature, wind, type of charcoal, and the metal thickness of the smoker all affect the time. Time guidelines are provided in the following recipes but only *you* can tell if it is done. Opening the smoker should be avoided until the minimum time is up since smoke and heat escape quickly. A fast check at that time will indicate if all is well. The leg on a game bird should move easily when wiggled back and forth; the thigh is the last part of the bird to cook. If the breast or thigh meat is still a bit pink when cut into, that's all right. There is no reason to overcook game birds. When the game is cooked, no harm is done if it is left in the smoker for another half hour or so. With a charcoal smoker, the coals will be cooling;

in a propane model, turn the heat to low. In an electric smoker, move the game farther away from the heat, if possible.

The dry-heat electric smoker usually has a very thin-gauge aluminum shell which makes it difficult to use in cold weather. The way to overcome this problem is to retain the packing box. The smoker can be encased in its carton for extra insulation. Cut a slot at the bottom of the box so the sawdust pan can be refilled easily. I've used my electric smoker this way for several winters and it works beautifully.

Don't forget to smoke your fish too. I find the dry-heat smokers especially valuable for fish. Just don't overcook them. They are best to eat when a little moisture is left in them.

Tip: Keep the manufacturer's directions with the smoker, then they'll be handy each time it is used. After a piece of game is smoked, make a couple of notes on how long it took and what the weather conditions were (temperature and wind). Each smoker is different and these notes will be valuable the next time the same bird or animal is smoked. Note: If the smoker has a gauge, try to keep the temperature on the line between the "low" and "ideal" range for moist gamebirds and animals.

Pheasant

> 1 or 2 birds with skin
> 1 tablespoon seasoned salt per bird
> Beer (enough to cover bird[s])
> Soft butter

Place the pheasant in a bowl and cover with beer. Cover and marinate in the refrigerator for 12 to 18 hours. If the bird(s) aren't completely covered with the liquid, turn them several times during the period. Dry the pheasant on paper towels, wiping the moisture off the skin. Carefully work your finger tips under the breast skin, starting at the tip of the breast bone. When the skin is loose, push about ½ tablespoon of seasoned salt between the skin and the breast. Sprinkle the rest of the seasoned salt in the cavity. Rub the entire bird with soft butter and either hang the bird in the smoker (if it is so equipped) or place on a well-oiled rack. If a moist-heat smoker is used, pour the beer marinade in the water pan and add water until it is almost full. Smoke according to the manufacturer's directions. My pheasants usually take about 6 hours. 3 to 4 pans of sawdust in the dry-heat smoker will be about right for a nice, smoky flavor.

• • • • •

Grouse

2 grouse with skin
1 cup red wine
1 cup water
$\frac{1}{4}$ cup salt
$\frac{1}{4}$ cup brown sugar
$\frac{1}{4}$ teaspoon pepper
1 garlic clove, minced
2 slices of onion
Soft butter

Mix wine, water, salt, sugar, pepper, garlic, and onion in a saucepan and heat until it reaches the boiling point. Turn the heat down to simmer and cook for 5 minutes. Cool the marinade until it is room temperature. Place the grouse in a nonmetal bowl and cover with marinade, adding more water if necessary to cover the birds. Cover the bowl and refrigerate for 8 to 10 hours. Dry the grouse thoroughly on paper towels and rub them all over with soft butter. Smoke according to the smoker's directions. I find that grouse usually take about 4 to 5 hours (using 3 pans of sawdust in the dry-heat model). Use the marinade in the water pan in the moist-heat smoker, adding more water.

• • • • •

Duck

2 ducks with skin
Water to cover
$\frac{1}{2}$ cup salt
$\frac{1}{2}$ cup brown sugar
Soft butter

In a nonmetal bowl, mix the water, salt, and sugar until everything has dissolved. Add the ducks to the bowl and more water, if necessary to cover the birds. Cover the bowl and refrigerate for 24 hours. Drain the ducks thoroughly on paper towels, wiping the skin well. Rub the skin with butter and place on a well-oiled rack in the smoker. Smoke according to the manufacturer's directions for about 5 hours. Place water in the water pan of the moist-heat smoker *or* when using the dry-heat model, try 3 pans of sawdust for good results.

• • • • •

Goose

>   1 wild goose with skin
>   2 cups canning salt
>   1 cup white sugar
> $\frac{1}{4}$ teaspoon garlic powder
> $1\frac{1}{2}$ tablespoons pickling spices

Mix salt, sugar, garlic powder, and pickling spices in a saucepan with a quart of water. Bring to a boil, lower heat to simmer, and cook for 5 minutes. Cool to room temperature. Place the goose in a large nonmetal bowl and cover with brine, adding more cold water to cover the bird. Cover the bowl and refrigerate for 36 to 48 hours. Rinse the goose well in cold water, inside and out. Dry well with paper towels and air dry on a cookie sheet for 2 hours. Place the goose on a well-oiled rack in the smoker. Smoke according to the manufacturer's directions, for about 8 hours. Use 4 to 5 pans of sawdust in the dry-heat smoker. Add water to the water pan of the moist-heat smoker.

• • • • •

Woodcock

> 4 woodcock with skin
> Water
> $\frac{1}{3}$ cup salt
> $\frac{1}{3}$ cup white sugar
> 2 bay leaves
> $\frac{1}{2}$ teaspoon chili powder
> $\frac{1}{2}$ teaspoon black pepper

Mix salt, sugar, bay leaves, chili powder, and black pepper with 2 cups of water in a saucepan. Bring to a boil, reduce heat, and simmer for 10 minutes. Cool to room temperature. Place the birds in a nonmetal bowl and pour the marinade over them, adding more water if necessary to cover the woodcock. Cover and refrigerate for 8 to 10 hours. Dry the birds on paper towels and place on a well-oiled rack in the smoker. Smoke according to the manufacturer's directions, 3 to 4 hours. Use 2 pans of sawdust in the dry-heat smoker. Add the marinade to the water pan in the moist-heat model, adding more water.

• • • • •

Moist Smoked Venison

> 5$\frac{1}{2}$-pound venison leg roast
> 1 cup barbecue sauce
> 1 cup red wine
> 2 tablespoons cooking oil
> $\frac{1}{2}$ teaspoon chili powder

Mix barbecue sauce, wine, oil, and chili powder well. Place the roast in a roasting pan and pour the marinade over it. Turn the roast several times so the sauce completely coats it. Cover the pan and refrigerate for 24 hours. A couple of times during the period, turn the roast over in the marinade.

Buy $\frac{1}{2}$ to $\frac{3}{4}$ pound of clean beef suet from your meat market. Cut it into thin slabs, about $\frac{1}{4}$ to $\frac{1}{2}$ inch thick. Remove the meat from the marinade. Cover the roast with slices of suet, top and bottom. Use string to tie the suet to the roast. This is called larding and keeps the meat moist while it is smoking.

Start the moist-heat smoker according to manufacturer's directions. Place the marinade in the water pan and fill it with water. Grease the rack and lay the larded roast on it. Cover the smoker and cook for about 5 hours. If the smoker has a gauge, try to keep the heat on the line between "low" and "ideal" or in the lower "ideal" range. Don't open the cover until the time is nearly up. Serves 8 for dinner.

Serve with Hunt Sauce (see "Game Sauces" chapter) or with the juices in the water pan (remove the grease first).

Note: "Super recipe."

• • • • •

Smoked Venison & Spaghetti

> 1 to 1½ cups leftover moist smoked venison, cut into small, thin chunks (press meat firmly into the cup)
> ½ to ¾ cup leftover Hunt Sauce
> ¼ cup milk
> 2 tablespoons catsup
> 1 teaspoon cornstarch or arrowroot
> Cooked spaghetti
> Parmesan cheese
> Parsley sprigs

Slowly heat Hunt Sauce and venison chunks in a large, heavy saucepan. To stretch the sauce, place milk, catsup, and cornstarch (or arrowroot) in a small jar and shake well. Add to the Hunt Sauce and stir in well, heating until it boils. (This "stretching" mixture can be doubled if you wish.) Cook enough spaghetti for four small servings. Toss the cooked spaghetti with the hot sauce and meat and serve with grated cheese. Garnish with parsley.

Serves 4. For a hearty meal, serve with Italian bread and a green salad.

Note: "Great recipe."

• • • • •

Chili Venison Sandwiches

Leftover smoked venison, cut into very thin pieces
Chili sauce
Hamburger rolls

Place the leftover meat in a frying pan and moisten with enough chili sauce to make a "Sloppy Joe" type sandwich. Heat well and serve on warm hamburger rolls. Servings depend on the amount of meat. $\frac{1}{3}$ cup of meat will make one hearty sandwich (press the meat firmly in the measuring cup).

• • • • •

Smoked Pâté

1 cup ground smoked meat
$\frac{1}{4}$ teaspoon onion powder
1 cup soft butter
2 tablespoons brandy

Cut meat from wings, legs, and back of smoked birds. Put through a meat grinder. Mix the meat with onion powder, butter, and brandy. Use the back of a wooden spoon to mix thoroughly. Serve with crackers as a snack or appetizer.

Odds & Ends

Wild game is too valuable to throw away. Discarding wings, legs, backbones, necks, hearts, livers, and gizzards is near criminal behavior and yet this happens frequently. Every year as habitat is reduced we have fewer and fewer opportunities to fill our game pouches. Therefore, we must get the most out of every bit we bring home.

As a for instance, let's take a pheasant. In the section covering that bird I suggest the best way to cook pheasant and to stretch it into several meals is to fillet the breast meat off the bone for one meal; then cut off the legs for another recipe. The next step is to cut the carcass into manageable pieces with game scissors and store it (with the giblets) in the freezer for the recipes in this section. I use a large, heavy plastic bag (Ziploc) that is labeled "odds & ends" and keep adding to it until I have enough for a pot of stew or soup or whatever.

It's perfectly all right to mix species in this bag; in fact it adds fun, adventure, and flavor to the finished dish. I can't imagine a more exciting dish than a combination of dove, duck, woodcock, and goose. Add a few giblets and you have a true, migratory, wild-game potpourri.

If you don't use all of your game birds, shame on you. They are full of flavor, packed with protein, low in fat, and best of all, free (well, almost).

Game Stew

    2 cups cooked meat★ (from backs, legs, liver, hearts, etc.)
    ¼ cup finely chopped celery
    ¼ cup finely chopped onion
    ¼ cup finely chopped green pepper
    ¼ cup finely chopped carrot
    3 tablespoons cooking oil
    3 tablespoons flour
    1½ cups broth from cooking meat
    ½ cup finely chopped tomato
    1 tablespoon steak sauce
    ½ teaspoon savory
      Salt & pepper to taste
      Parsley sprigs

★Cover meat and bones with water in a large pot. Add a little salt and pepper, a bay leaf, some celery leaves and a slice of onion. Simmer until tender. Cool slightly, remove bones, and cut meat into small cubes. Strain broth and use in recipe.

In a frying pan, heat oil and fry celery, onion, green pepper, and carrot until they are tender but not too brown, about 10 minutes. Add flour to pan and stir. Gradually add broth, stirring constantly. Add tomato, steak sauce, and savory. Simmer for 5 minutes. Add meat and taste the sauce. Correct salt and pepper, if necessary. Heat thoroughly. Serve by ladling over hot, buttered rice or toast. Garnish with parsley. Makes 4 large servings or 6 small ones.

Note: "Very good recipe."

• • • • •

Small Game Potpourri

> Legs from 3 pheasants, or 6 grouse, or 12 quail (or 2 to 3 whole squirrels, cut into serving pieces or 1 rabbit)
> 1 cup dry red wine
> 1 teaspoon sugar
> $\frac{1}{4}$ cup wine vinegar
> $\frac{1}{8}$ teaspoon garlic powder
> Pinch of red pepper
> 2 tablespoons butter
> 2 tablespoons cooking oil
> 1 onion, sliced
> Flour
> Salt & pepper
> 2 tablespoons tomato paste
> 1 cup small whole mushrooms

Put the wine, sugar, vinegar, garlic powder, and red pepper in a saucepan and heat to the boiling point. Cool slightly. Place the game pieces in a nonmetal bowl and cover with the marinade (above mixture). Add a little water if necessary to cover game. Marinate for 4 hours, turning the game once.

Heat the butter and cooking oil in a large frying pan and fry the onion over medium heat for 5 minutes. Push the onion slices up the sides of the pan. Remove the game from the marinade and dry on paper towels. Roll in the flour seasoned with a little salt and pepper. Brown on all sides in the hot butter/oil over medium-high heat. Add tomato paste to the marinade and stir. Add the mixture to the frying pan and bring to a boil. Turn the game pieces and onion over in the mixture, add the mushrooms, cover, and turn the heat to simmer. Cook until tender. Time depends on the species—quail take the shortest time, about $\frac{1}{2}$ hour; old pheasant legs may take up to $1\frac{3}{4}$ hours. Serves 4.

Note: "Absolutely great recipe."

• • • • •

Giblet Dip

> 1½ cups cooked giblet and neck meat★
> ¼ cup giblet broth (more or less)
> 1½ tablespoons Madeira or sherry
> ¼ cup sour cream

★Place meat in a large saucepan and cover with water. Add a bay leaf, salt, pepper, and 1 chicken bouillon cube. Cover and simmer until all is tender. Cool slightly and cut into tiny pieces, removing all bones, skin, etc. Save ¼ cup broth for recipe and freeze the rest for use in soup and stews.

Place meat with enough broth (about ¼ cup) to moisten in a blender or processor. Puree until smooth, adding more broth if necessary. Put pureed meat in a bowl and blend in Madeira or sherry and sour cream. Serve warm as a dip with crackers or chill and serve as a cracker spread.

Note: "Very good."

• • • • •

Duck Soup

> Wings, legs, and backs from 2 large ducks or 4
>   small ones, or 1 goose
> 4 cups water
> 1 rib celery
> 1 chunked onion
> 1 teaspoon rosemary
> Salt & pepper to taste
> 6 medium carrots, chunked
> 4 cups broth from cooking meat
> 1 cup light cream (half & half, or mix equal parts of
>   whipping cream & milk)
> 4 tablespoons butter
> 4 tablespoons Madeira
> ⅛ teaspoon red pepper
> Chopped parsley

Cook the meat in water with celery, onion, rosemary, and a little salt and pepper. Cover and simmer until the meat falls from the bones, from 1½ to 3 hours, depending on the age of the bird(s). Add carrots when 30 minutes of cooking time remains and cook until tender. Remove meat from bones and cut into small pieces.

Place the meat and carrots in a blender with a little of the broth (about ¼ cup) and puree. Strain the rest of the broth, add enough water to measure 4 cups, and place in a large saucepan. Add the meat/carrot puree, cream, butter, Madeira, and red pepper. Mix and simmer for 5 minutes. Taste and correct salt and pepper. Serve garnished with chopped parsley. Will serve 6 to 8.

Note: "Great soup."

• • • • •

Odds & Ends Game Soup

This soup is lots of fun as well as economical. All your odds and ends of game can be used as well as leftover vegetables from the refrigerator. Onion, celery, cabbage, tomato, and carrots are the necessary vegetables; others can be added if you wish.

    1 large beef soup bone
      Water to cover
      Game odds & ends (legs, wings, carcasses, liver, hearts, etc.)
    1 large onion, chopped
    3 ribs celery with leaves, chopped
    1 2-inch wedge of cabbage, chopped
    1 large tomato or 1 small can
    3 large carrots, chopped

Optional

>   2 small potatoes, chopped
>   Corn
>   Lima beans
>   Peas
>   Broccoli
>   Cauliflower
>   Other vegetables

Place the soup bone in a large, deep pot and cover with water. Add a little salt and pepper. Cover and simmer for about 8 hours. (I like to start the soup the evening before, then put it in the refrigerator overnight. First thing in the morning, I remove the fat that has congealed on the top and then simmer the soup for another 4 hours.) Remove the soup bone and add the game scraps. Simmer for 2 to 3 hours, covered, until all is tender.

Strain the broth to remove bones, shot, etc. Put broth back in the pot and add onion, celery, cabbage, and tomato. Taste the broth and add a little more salt and pepper if necessary. Cover and simmer for 2 hours.

Remove the meat from the bones and cut into small pieces. Add carrots to the broth and cook 5 minutes. Add rest of vegetables and cook just until they are tender, about 15 minutes. If they are cooked too much, the soup will be mushy, especially if the soup is frozen for a time. When the vegetables are tender, add the meat and any leftover cooked vegetables. Heat and serve.

The soup can be stored in the freezer for a month or in the refrigerator for 4 days. If frozen, allow it to thaw partially before heating.

Note: "Excellent."

•   •   •   •   •

Mixed Bag Stew

A combination of legs, wings, and backs from game birds & small animals (pheasant, grouse, chukar, squirrel, rabbit, etc.)

                2   tablespoons butter
                3   slices fatty bacon
                    Flour
                $\frac{1}{4}$ cup water
                $\frac{1}{2}$ cup red wine
        16 oz. (2 cups) canned tomatoes, chopped
                $\frac{1}{2}$ teaspoon savory
                $\frac{1}{2}$ teaspoon thyme
                $\frac{1}{2}$ teaspoon salt
                    Pepper to taste
                1   teaspoon sugar
                4   small onions
                1   cup sliced mushrooms

Melt butter in a Dutch oven. Chop bacon into small pieces and brown in the butter. Roll the game pieces (enough to serve four people) in flour and brown on all sides in the hot fat. Add the water, wine, tomatoes, savory, thyme, salt, pepper, and sugar to the pot and mix well. Add more water if necessary to cover game. Bring the stew to a boil, cover, lower heat to simmer, and cook until all is tender. Add the onions and mushrooms 30 minutes before the cooking time is up. With a slotted spoon, lift the game out of the Dutch oven, cool slightly, and strip the meat from the bones. The stew can be thickened by sprinkling Quick Mixing flour over the stew, stirring, and heating until the broth starts to thicken. Return the meat to the stew, stir and serve. This stew can be cooked early in the day and reheated before serving time.

Note: "Very good."

• • • • •

Pheasant Soup

> 2 pheasant backbones and wings
> Slice of onion
> Hunk of carrot
> Celery leaves
> Noodles
> Salt & pepper to taste
> Vegetables (optional)

Place pheasant, onion, carrot, and celery in a pot with enough water to cover the bones. Simmer until the pheasant is tender. Remove the pheasant from the broth with a slotted spoon. Cool slightly and strip the meat from the bones.

Strain the broth to remove bone chips, shot, and vegetables. Cook the broth down over high heat until you have about 4 cups left. Throw a handful of noodles into the broth and cook according to the package directions. If you wish, just before the noodles are cooked, add a few leftover vegetables to the pot—peas, corn, or broccoli buds are good. Taste the broth and correct salt & pepper after it has been reduced. Before serving, add cooked pheasant meat. Will serve 4.

Note: "Easy and delicious."

•　•　•　•　•

Sourdough

I've worked with sourdough several times over the past ten years and find it is fun and rewarding. From the amount of mail I received from *Field & Stream* readers after a sourdough article, I have to conclude that a lot of people feel the same way I do. Nothing tastes much better during cold weather than baked goods made the sourdough way. Best of all, it seems to go with game dishes in a way that overshadows ordinary bread, probably because of the outdoor tradition that is connected with sourdough. Our pioneers managed to carry their starters across the country in wagon trains and relied on the bread to supplement their rations during lean days.

Sourdough fanciers love to brag about how old their starter is. One is reputed to date from the Alaskan gold-rush days. I'm daring to break with this tradition and say it's a bit of a pain to keep the starter when it isn't being used. It has to be "fed" regularly and can still go bad. I've been making my starter whenever I want to bake. When I've filled the freezer with baked goodies, I simply throw the starter away. It's a lot easier than worrying about it, especially if you are on vacation. Some people even have sourdough sitters! I think that's silly when it's so easy to make a new batch.

One of the rules of the sourdough game that I do follow is to never use metal when working with the dough. I use wooden spoons and glass or crockery bowls. Another rule is that everything that goes into sourdough should be warm, not cold from the refrigerator. Both metal and cold kill the sourdough action.

While it is working and rising, sourdough needs a warm place (between 85°F. and 100°F.) to bubble and sour. In modern houses, this is often hard to find. I solved the problem by using a heating pad. With the cover on the pad and the setting turned to medium, the temperature is 90°F. Other alternatives are the top of a radiator (with a layer of magazines), radio or television set, or the oven of a gas range (the pilot light provides warmth). Check different places with a thermometer until the right spot is located.

Kneading is something most of us learn to do by watching our mothers as kids. The reason you knead dough is to thoroughly mix the flour into the stiff batter. While watching someone knead is still the best way to learn; I'll attempt to describe it. The dough is scraped out of the bowl onto a floured board when it is no longer possible to mix with a wooden spoon. Flour your hands and gather the mass into a clumsy mound. Then punch the palms of your hands into the mound putting your arms and shoulders into the task. Next, lift one side of the dough up and to one side slightly (use either hand depending on whether you are right or left handed, or even both hands). Punch down again with both palms. With the right lift movement, your punches will go into the dough at a different place each time. Set up a regular rhythm of punch—lift—punch—lift. The dough will be transformed from an unyielding mess into a smooth, shiny, elastic ball in 8 to 10 minutes. Add more flour to the board as necessary to keep the dough from sticking. Good kneading leads to a nice bread texture.

I've listed two recipes for sourdough bread because the loaves are so different—one is hearty and other is light; both are very good. The first recipe gives me a nicely textured, hearty bread that browns beautifully and toasts to a glorious, golden color. The San Francisco bread has great texture and is very light.

Sourdough baking always starts with the blending of a "starter."

Sourdough Starter

>   3 cups warm water
>   1 package dry yeast
>   3 cups unbleached white flour (or whole wheat flour)

Place the water in a nonmetal bowl or crock. Sprinkle dry yeast over it and allow it to soften and dissolve (about 5 minutes). Mix well, then add flour, 1 cup at a time. Stir with wooden spoon until it is well blended. Cover the bowl with a towel and place in a warm (85 to 100°F.) spot. Stir starter several times while it is working. By the end of 48 hours, it should be bubbly and smell sour. Mix well before using. After using, replenish the starter with equal amounts of warm water and flour—if you have removed 1 cup of starter, add 1 cup warm water and 1 cup flour and stir well. Set in the warm spot for several hours. If you wish to store the starter, cover with plastic wrap and place in the refrigerator between uses. A couple hours before it is needed, remove from the refrigerator and place in warm spot. Once a week, if it isn't used, throw half of the starter away, add 1½ cups warm water and 1½ cups of flour to the rest, mix well, and set it in the warm place for several hours until it is bubbly and active again.

Sourdough starters sometimes have minds of their own. If yours doesn't act like it should, throw it away and start over again. Each batch is slightly different and the baked goods made from it will be different too. That's why there is some leeway in the amount of flour in the recipes.

Sourdough Bread
(2 loaves)

Sponge:

>   2 cups sourdough starter
>   2 cups unbleached flour
>   1 cup warm water

The night before baking, mix the starter, flour, and water. Place in a greased bowl, cover with a damp towel, and place in a warm place.

Dough:

- ½ cup warm water
- 2 packages dry yeast
- 4 tablespoons sugar
- 2 teaspoons salt
- ½ cup cooking oil
- 4 to 6 cups unbleached flour (amount depends on humidity, altitude, and wateriness of starter)

Place the warm water in a nonmetal bowl and sprinkle dry yeast on it. Allow the yeast to soften and dissolve for about 5 minutes. Then add sponge, sugar, salt, and cooking oil and mix well. Add flour, 1 cup at a time, until it's difficult to stir with the wooden spoon. Turn out on a well-floured board and knead for about 8 to 10 minutes, until the dough is smooth, shiny, and elastic. Incorporate more flour until the dough no longer sticks to your fingers when it is lifted.

Place the dough in a well-oiled bowl and turn the dough once to grease the top. Allow to rise until double in a warm place, covered with a damp towel. This will take 1½ to 2 hours.

Turn the dough onto a lightly floured board. Divide the dough into two parts. Knead each half briefly, about 1 to 2 minutes. Shape into loaf shape and place in 2 well-oiled loaf pans. Brush the top with melted butter, cover with a damp towel, and place in a warm place to double in size—about ¾ to 1 hour (don't allow loaves to rise more than double or they will have air holes—the loaves will rise more in the oven). When it has almost doubled, use a very sharp knife to slash the top of the loaves in three or four places so they will bake evenly and not split. Place the loaves in a cold oven and turn the heat to 375°F. Bake for 50 to 55 minutes until the bottom of the loaves sounds hollow when tapped with fingers. If you're unsure, insert a toothpick in the middle of the bottom. It should come out clean if the bread is done. Brush the top of the loaves with melted butter and allow them to cool on a rack (out of the loaf pans) in a breeze-free area.

Because it has no preservatives, homemade bread spoils quicker than commercial bread. When cool, wrap the bread in aluminum foil and keep in the refrigerator. Extra loaves should be well wrapped and stored in the freezer. This recipe makes 2 loaves.

1 cup of whole wheat flour may be substituted for 1 cup of the white flour in both the sponge and dough recipes.

• • • • •

San Francisco Sourdough Bread
(2 loaves)

Sponge:

> 1 cup starter
> 1 cup unbleached white flour
> 1 cup warm water

The night before baking, mix the starter, water, and flour. Cover with a damp towel and place the bowl in a warm spot.

Dough:

> 1 package dry yeast
> $\frac{1}{2}$ cup warm water
> $\frac{1}{2}$ teaspoon honey
> 1 teaspoon salt
> $2\frac{1}{2}$ to $3\frac{1}{2}$ cups unbleached white flour
> Sesame seeds or poppy seeds (optional)
> Melted butter

Mix yeast, warm water, and honey until the yeast is soft and dissolved. In a large bowl, mix the sponge, yeast mixture, salt, and flour, adding one cup of flour at a time. Turn the dough out on a heavily floured board when it becomes too difficult to mix in the bowl. Knead for 8 to 10 minutes, incorporating more flour until the dough no longer sticks to the hands. The dough should be shiny, smooth, and elastic.

Place the dough in a well-oiled bowl, turning once to coat the top with oil. Cover with a damp towel and place in a warm place (85 to 100°F.) until double in size, about 1 hour. Punch the dough down and turn out on a lightly floured surface. Knead for

1 to 2 minutes. Cut dough in half and shape into 2 long, thin loaves. Oil 2 French loaf pans and sprinkle with white cornmeal. (I don't have these pans so I used a cookie sheet treated the same way.) Place the loaves in the pans or on the sheet. To keep the loaves on the sheet from spreading too much, make them thin and about 10 inches long, pulling the dough upwards to encourage it to rise this way.

Brush the loaves generously with melted butter, cover with a damp towel, and place in a warm spot for about 45 minutes. Don't allow the bread dough to rise more than double. Watch the towel so it doesn't stick to the top of the loaves (if it happens, use a knife to gently free it). When the bread is almost double, use a sharp knife to slash the top of the loaves about 2 inches apart. If the loaves are close together, brush with more butter so they will break apart easily once they are baked. Sprinkle loaves with seeds if you wish. Place in a cold oven and turn the heat to 425°F. Bake for about 25 minutes until the loaves sound hollow when tapped on the bottom. For a soft crust, brush again with melted butter. Cool on a wire rack in a draft-free place. To store, wrap in aluminum foil and refrigerate or freeze.

• • • • •

Muffins

1 egg, beaten
½ cup light cream (room temperature)—use half & half
    or mix equal parts whipping cream and milk
2 cups unbleached white flour
½ cup sugar
1 teaspoon salt
1 teaspoon baking soda
1 teaspoon baking powder
½ cup cooking oil
½ cup chopped walnuts
½ cup raisins
½ cup sourdough starter

Mix egg and cream. Sift flour, sugar, salt, baking soda, and baking powder into a large bowl. Add egg mixture and cooking oil and mix well. Stir in walnuts and raisins. Add starter and fold into the batter just until it is incorporated. Don't over mix. (To fold, gently and slowly cut through the ingredients with the wooden spoon in an up and down motion rolling the spoon as it goes through the batter.) Ladle the batter into well-greased muffin pan and bake at 375°F. for 20 to 25 minutes, until a toothpick inserted into the center of the largest muffin comes out clean. Makes 10 to 12 muffins, depending on the size you wish.

Serving Suggestion: These are the greatest muffins in the world. They are perfect for breakfast. You can freeze them and then pop them in a toaster oven to warm. Serve with lots of butter.

• • • • •

Coffee Cake

$\frac{3}{4}$ cup flour
$\frac{1}{2}$ teaspoon salt
$\frac{1}{4}$ cup sugar
$\frac{1}{2}$ teaspoon baking soda
1 egg
$\frac{1}{4}$ cup cooking oil
2 tablespoons milk
$\frac{1}{4}$ teaspoon vanilla
1 cup sourdough starter

Sift flour, salt, sugar, and soda together in one bowl. In a second bowl, beat egg and add oil, milk, and vanilla and mix well. Add warm starter and mix lightly. Then mix liquid ingredients into the flour mixture until blended. Don't over mix. Pour the batter into a greased 9-by-9-inch cake pan (or any similar-size, round baking dish). Sprinkle Topping (recipe below) on the batter and bake in a preheated 400°F. oven for about 25 minutes or until a toothpick comes out clean when inserted in the middle of the cake.

Topping:

$\frac{1}{2}$ cup sugar
3 tablespoons flour
2 teaspoons cinnamon
$\frac{1}{4}$ cup chopped walnuts
2 tablespoons melted butter

Mix all ingredients together and sprinkle evenly on coffee cake batter.

•　•　•　•　•

Pancakes

2 cups sourdough starter
1$\frac{1}{4}$ cup flour
1 cup milk
1 well-beaten egg
3 tablespoons sugar
$\frac{1}{2}$ teaspoon baking soda
$\frac{1}{2}$ teaspoon salt
2 tablespoons melted butter

Take the starter out of the refrigerator and add flour and milk. Mix well in a bowl, cover lightly, and place in a warm place over night. The next morning, stir in the egg, sugar, soda, salt, and butter. Don't beat, just mix. If the batter is too thick, add a little milk; if too thin, sift a couple tablespoons of flour into it. Allow batter to stand a few minutes, then spoon on a hot griddle and cook like regular pancakes. Makes about 24 thin pancakes.

To cut recipe in half, the egg can be beaten and then half used or the whole egg may be used for a richer batter. To cut flour in half, measure out $\frac{1}{2}$ cup plus 2 tablespoons.

•　•　•　•　•

Biscuits

 1¾ to 2 cups flour
 ½ teaspoon baking soda
 1½ teaspoons baking powder
 1 tablespoon sugar
 ½ teaspoon salt
 ½ cup milk (room temperature)
 1 tablespoon melted butter
 ½ cup warm sourdough starter

Sift 1¾ cups flour with baking soda, baking powder, sugar, and salt in a bowl. Mix milk, butter, and sourdough starter in another bowl and add to the dry ingredients. Add more sifted flour if necessary to form a stiff dough. Turn the dough out on a floured board and knead with fingers just until the flour is incorporated. Pat the dough out until it is about ½ inch thick. Use a floured fruit glass or biscuit cutter to cut the biscuits. Place biscuits on a baking sheet, brush with melted butter, and bake in a preheated 425°F. oven for about 10 minutes. Makes 12 to 15 biscuits.

• • • • •

Skillet Corn Bread

 1½ cups uncooked yellow cornmeal
 1¾ cups diluted evaporated milk (half evaporated milk
    and half water)
 2 eggs
 3 tablespoons sugar
 ¼ cup melted butter or margarine
 ¾ teaspoon salt
 ¾ teaspoon baking soda
 1 cup sourdough starter

Combine cornmeal and milk in a mixing bowl. Add eggs and sugar and beat well. Add melted butter, salt, and soda (be sure all lumps are out of the baking soda) and mix. Add starter and blend.

Pour the batter into a greased, heavy, oven-proof skillet, one that is about 10 inches in diameter (I use an iron skillet). Bake in a preheated hot oven (450°F.) until the bread is crusty and brown, about 25 to 30 minutes. A toothpick inserted at the center should come out clean. Serve hot, cut into wedges. Serves 8 to 10.

• • • • •

Game Sauces

Sauces should be reasonably easy to prepare and complement the main dish, not overpower it. For instance, a delicate sauce (such as "3 M Sauce" or "Blackberry Game Sauce") goes well with most grouse, quail, or pheasant breast recipes, or steak and chops done to the medium-rare stage. A rich, more complicated (in taste) sauce is often served with woodcock, duck, goose, or big game ("Hunt Sauce" and "Easy Chasseur Sauce" are examples). The game must stand out, not be overwhelmed. Well-cleaned and well-cooked game should not need to be disguised, but enhanced with a sauce. "Creamy Mushroom Sauce" and "Lime Marmalade Sauce" can be served with any wild dish.

Most sauces can be prepared $\frac{1}{2}$ an hour or so before dinner. Then, at the last minute, reheat it over low heat. If it's a bit too thick, stir in a little water (or milk in cream sauces) to thin it. This isn't the classic way to make sauces but it sure does save the "cook's prance" when you're trying to do everything at once. Each recipe in this chapter contains hints for do-ahead preparation.

3 M Sauce

> 1 green onion, minced
> 1 cup chopped mushrooms
> 3 tablespoons butter
> 1 beef bouillon cube
> 1 tablespoon Dijon-style mustard
> 1 teaspoon lemon juice
> 2 tablespoons Madeira wine
> ¾ cup cold water
> 1 tablespoon arrowroot (or cornstarch)

Cook onion and mushrooms in butter over medium-high heat in a medium-size skillet. Fry until tender, about 5 to 7 minutes. Put the bouillon cube in the pan and crush it with the back of a spoon. Place the mustard, lemon juice, Madeira, water, and arrowroot in a large jar, cover, and shake until it is well mixed. This part of the recipe can be accomplished ½ hour or so before dinner. At the last minute, reheat the onion/mushroom mixture to the boiling point, add the contents of the jar (after shaking again) and stir until the sauce bubbles. Serves 4.

Note: "Great."

• • • • •

Easy Chasseur Sauce

> 2 beef bouillon cubes
> 1½ cups water
> Cheesecloth bag containing celery leaves, 1 bay leaf, 1 slice of onion, 1 sprig of parsley, and 2 slices of carrot
> 1 pinch each of thyme, allspice, marjoram, tarragon, and garlic powder
> ½ cup sliced mushrooms
> 1 green onion, minced
> 2 tablespoons butter
> 2 tablespoons flour
> 2 teaspoons tomato paste
> ¼ cup white wine
> 1 tablespoon minced parsley
> Pepper

Tie contents of cheesecloth (double thickness) closed with string. Place the bag and water with the bouillon cubes, herbs, and spices in a saucepan. Bring to a boil, lower heat to simmer, and cook for 20 minutes, stirring occasionally. Remove the cheesecloth bag from the broth, squeezing the juice from the bag. Measure broth and add enough white wine to make 1 cup. At this point, the recipe can be held for several hours or even days. Refrigerate the broth covered.

Brown mushrooms and onion in butter in a skillet. Add flour and mix. Slowly add the broth, stirring constantly. Add tomato paste and ¼ cup white wine and mix thoroughly. Simmer for 5 minutes and add pepper if you wish (taste first). Add parsley and serve. Serves 4 to 6.

Note: "Super on steaks or chops."

• • • • •

Blackberry Game Sauce

> 4 cups washed blackberries
> ½ lemon
> ½ lime
> 1 cup sugar
> 1 cup liquid pectin

Mince the lemon and lime (after removing seeds) until the rinds are in very small bits. Put them, with the berries, in a large pot and bring to a boil. Cook over moderate heat for 30 minutes. Add sugar and cook another 30 minutes. Remove from heat, add 1 cup of liquid pectin and pour into hot, sterilized jars. Seal with paraffin.

Note: "Nice tart sauce that can be made when blackberries are in season."

• • • • •

Hunt Sauce

> 1 carrot, finely chopped
> 1 medium onion, finely chopped
> 1 garlic clove, minced
> ¼ cup good olive oil (or cooking oil)
> 3 tablespoons catsup
> 2 beef bouillon cubes
> ¼ cup chopped, boiled ham
> ½ cup orange juice
> ⅔ cup whipping cream

Place carrot, onion, garlic, oil, catsup, bouillon cubes, and ham in a heavy skillet and cook over medium heat for about 25 minutes, stirring occasionally. The vegetables will turn brown. At this point the recipe can be held for a ½ hour or so. At the last minute, reheat the mixture and add orange juice and cream. Heat thoroughly and serve generously ladled over cooked pieces of game. Serves 4.

Note: "Super sauce—we have tried it on duck, goose, and venison."

• • • • •

Creamy Mushroom Sauce

> ½ cup sliced fresh mushrooms
> 3 tablespoons butter
> 2 tablespoons flour
> ¼ teaspoon seasoned salt
> ¼ teaspoon steak sauce
> ¼ teaspoon Kitchen Bouquet
> 1 cup light cream, more or less
> 1 tablespoon brandy

Fry mushrooms in the butter over medium-high heat until tender, about 7 minutes. Add flour, salt, steak sauce, and Kitchen Bouquet and stir. Blend in the light cream and brandy, stirring constantly until the sauce is the right consistency. Simmer for 1 minute and serve a generous dollop on each serving of game. Serves 4 to 6. The sauce can be made ½ hour before serving. Reheat at the last minute over medium heat, stirring constantly. Add a little milk or cream to thin the sauce if necessary.

Note: "Great for all kinds of game."

• • • • •

Lime Marmalade Sauce

¼ cup lime marmalade
¼ cup orange juice
¼ cup Madeira wine
2 tablespoons butter
¼ teaspoon orange rind
1½ tablespoons lime juice
1½ teaspoons cornstarch

Put marmalade, orange juice, Madeira, butter, and rind in a small saucepan and heat until the butter is melted and the mixture hot. The recipe can be completed to this stage ½ hour or so before dinner. Before proceeding, reheat the mixture.

Mix the lime juice and cornstarch until the cornstarch is dissolved. Add to the hot sauce, stirring constantly until it thickens. Serves 4 to 6 (a little goes a long way).

Note: "Semisweet and fruity—great with duck, woodcock, and venison chops."

• • • • •

Dishes to Accompany Game

Side dishes should be easy, colorful, and taste good. The game should be the star attraction and the rest of the meal complement it. Simplicity is the answer, especially for beginning cooks.

Timing side dishes is always a problem: the seemingly impossible task of having everything done at the right time. You can make it easy on yourself with some planning. If the main dish is to be cooked on top of the stove, accompany it with an oven-baked vegetable. If the entree is baked or roasted, you'll have more time to fool around cooking side dishes on top of the stove. Many of the recipes in this section can be partially prepared ahead of time and then finished at the last minute before serving. Hints for doing this are included with the recipes.

Pay attention to the color of side dishes when planning meals. A pleasing combination on a dinner plate makes everything taste better since it appeals to other senses besides taste and smell. That's why I've included carrots, broccoli, zucchini, and tomatoes in these recipes. There are ways to pretty up other dishes like baked potatoes and wild rice. A sprinkling of paprika on potatoes and chopped fresh parsley on wild rice adds the needed sparkle. A sprig or two of parsley or watercress is always a welcome addition to a plate no matter how attractive it already looks. Picture a plate of "Pheasant Madeira" on a mound of rice with "Broiled Garden Tomatoes" as the vegetable. Then think how much better it will look with a little parsley added.

Tip: To keep parsley or watercress fresh and crisp in the refrigerator for a week or more, remove about $\frac{1}{2}$ inch of the stem bottoms and place the greens upright in a glass of cold water. Then cover the whole bundle with a plastic bag and refrigerate. Change the water every three or four days.

Vegetables that are frozen in plastic pouches, while expensive, are very handy for beginning game cooks, especially when the main dish requires last-minute preparation. The vegetable pouch is usually placed in boiling water for about 15 minutes and then served—no watching or checking for doneness. If you wish, the vegetables can be spruced up with a pinch of herbs or spices. For instance, a shake of cinnamon (don't use too much) adds a special touch to frozen peas.

Vegetable Dip

> $\frac{1}{3}$ cup mayonnaise
> 2 tablespoons prepared mustard
> 1 teaspoon steak sauce
> 2 teaspoons lemon juice
> 5 drops Tabasco sauce

Mix all the ingredients together thoroughly, cover, and chill for at least 4 hours before serving with vegetables. This dip is excellent with one or more of several vegetables: carrots, celery, cucumber, or zucchini sticks, radishes, cherry tomatoes, cauliflower chunks, small whole mushrooms, or green onions. The vegetables can be cut ahead of time and crisped for an hour in ice water.

Tip: This dip is especially good as an appetizer before a heavy meal such as duck, goose, or liver.

Note: "Excellent."

• • • • •

Avocado & Pear Salad

    1 large, whole, ripe avocado
    1 large pear (or canned slices)
    ⅓ cup mayonnaise
  1½ tablespoons peanut butter
      Salt & pepper
    4 lettuce leaves

Arrange each leaf on a salad plate (my favorite lettuce for this salad is either bibb or romaine). Peel and thinly slice the avocado and divide equally, arranging artfully on the lettuce. Peel and slice the pear and put between the avocado slices. In a small bowl, mix the mayonnaise and peanut butter. Spoon equally on the avocados and pears. Sprinkle with a little salt and pepper if desired and serve. Serves 4.

Note: "My favorite game salad—especially good with gamebirds."

• • • • •

Blue Cheese Salad

    3 tablespoons peanut oil
    1 tablespoon wine vinegar
    1 tablespoon crumbled blue cheese
      Salt & pepper
      Pinch of garlic powder
      Lettuce

In a small jar put the oil, vinegar, blue cheese, and a little salt and pepper with the garlic powder. Cover and shake vigorously. Allow to sit for 30 minutes, shake again, and dribble over enough torn lettuce for 4 helpings. Toss well and serve immediately. (Use something besides iceburg lettuce for best results.)

Note: "Simple and delicious."

• • • • •

Cucumber Salad

2 large cucumbers with skin
2 tablespoons wine vinegar
¼ cup sour cream
Salt & pepper

Thinly slice the cucumbers and place in a bowl. Mix the wine vinegar and sour cream with a little salt and pepper. Toss with the cucumbers until all is well mixed. Cover the bowl and refrigerate for 30 minutes. Remove from the refrigerator, toss lightly, and pour off the excessive moisture. Serve with a little additional pepper sprinkled on the top. Serves 4.

Note: "Very good."

• • • • •

My Thousand Island Salad

Lettuce
⅓ cup mayonnaise
3 tablespoons chili sauce
2 teaspoons horseradish
Salt & pepper

Mix the mayonnaise, chili sauce, and horseradish well and sprinkle with a little salt and pepper if desired. Break enough lettuce for 4 servings into bite-size pieces and toss with the dressing. Serve immediately, sprinkled with a little more pepper. Serves 4.

Note: "Simple and good."

• • • • •

Garden Tomato Salad

> 2 large garden tomatoes
> 2 tablespoons wine vinegar
> 1½ teaspoons sugar
>   Salt & pepper
>   Thyme

Peel the tomatoes and cut into thick slices. Arrange on a platter and dribble a little wine vinegar over them. Sprinkle with the sugar and a little salt, pepper, and thyme. Let sit at room temperature for 15 minutes before serving. Garnish platter with a sprig of parsley. Serves 4.

Note: "Very good."

• • • • •

Carrots & Mushrooms

> 3 carrots
> ½ cup sliced mushrooms
> 4 tablespoons butter
>   Salt & pepper
>   Pinch of savory

Thinly slice peeled carrots and place in a saucepan with enough water to cover. Bring to a boil, cover, and turn the heat to simmer for about 15 minutes, until they are tender but not over cooked.

Fry the sliced mushrooms in 1 tablespoon of the butter in a small skillet for about 7 minutes. (This can be done while the carrots are cooking or up to an hour ahead of time.)

Drain the carrots well and put the pan back over low heat. Add the mushrooms and 3 tablespoons of butter. Sprinkle with a little salt, pepper, and savory. Toss and heat until the butter is melted and everything is well heated. Serves 4.

Note: "Colorful and tasty."

• • • • •

Zucchini

> 2 medium-size zucchini
> 1 onion, chopped
> 2 tablespoons butter or margarine
> 2 tablespoons cooking oil
> Salt & pepper
> Grated Parmesan cheese

Grate the zucchini and place small handfuls of it in a tea towel. Squeeze the moisture out of the zucchini by wringing the towel in your hands over the sink. As each batch is done, place on several layers of paper towels. This can be done an hour or so before dinner.

Heat the butter and oil in a large skillet. Add the onion and fry over high heat for 3 minutes. Add the zucchini and fry for about 7 minutes, turning often with a spatula. It should be well browned but still crisp. Add a little salt and pepper while it is cooking. Just before serving, sprinkle with a little cheese and toss with the spatula. Serve immediately in a heated bowl. Serves 4.

Note: "Delicious."

• • • • •

Broiled Garden Tomatoes

> 4 tomatoes, peeled
> $\frac{1}{2}$ cup bread crumbs
> 3 tablespoons butter
> $\frac{1}{4}$ teaspoon onion powder
> 2 tablespoons Parmesan cheese
> 1 tablespoon chopped parsley

Cut each tomato in half and place on a piece of foil, covering a broiler pan. Melt the butter in a saucepan. Add the onion powder, bread crumbs, and cheese to the butter and toss until mixed. Sprinkle the mixture evenly over the tomatoes. (The recipe can be completed to this point 30 minutes or so before dinner.)

Place the broiler pan under a preheated broiler, about 4 inches from the heat, until the topping is brown. Lower the heat to 400°F. and cook (with the oven door closed) for about 7 minutes, until the tomatoes are a bit soft. Serve immediately, sprinkled with parsley. Serves 4.

Note: "Great."

• • • • •

Butternut Squash

>   2 medium-size butternut squashes
>   Butter
>   Salt & pepper

Scrub the squashes well and cut each in half, lengthwise. With a spoon scoop out the seeds and discard. Place the halves, right side up, in a roasting pan. Add about $\frac{1}{2}$ inch of water to the pan. Cover the squash with aluminum foil, sealing the sides. Place in a preheated 400°F. oven for about 1 hour, until the squash is very tender. Remove from the oven and place on a platter. Put a large chunk of butter in the cavity of each squash and sprinkle with salt and pepper. Serve with more butter. Serves 4 to 6.

Note: "Very easy and very good."

• • • • •

Browned Butter Spinach

>   1 pound package of fresh spinach
> $\frac{1}{4}$ cup butter

Wash spinach in cold water until all sand particles are gone. Remove tough stems and any spoiled pieces. Drain well and place in a large pot or skillet. Don't add any water; there is enough on the leaves to cook the spinach. Cover the pot and place over moderate heat for about 5 minutes, until the spinach is entirely wilted. Turn with a fork often so all the pieces of spinach get hot at the same time. While the spinach is cooking, place butter in a small saucepan and heat over medium-high temperature until it is brown. When the spinach is wilted, drain all moisture away pressing with the back of a wooden spoon to squeeze it from the leaves. Toss the spinach with the browned butter until it is well coated. Serves 4.

Note: "Excellent but easy dish."

• • • • •

Sautéed Cherry Tomatoes

> 2 dozen cherry tomatoes
> 2 tablespoons butter
> 2 tablespoons finely chopped parsley

Wash the tomatoes well in cold water. The stems can be removed. Dry the tomatoes well on paper towels. In a large skillet, heat the butter over medium-high heat. Add the tomatoes, turn the heat to high, and toss the tomatoes in the hot butter for 5 minutes. Sprinkle with parsley and serve immediately. Serves 4.

Note: "Beautiful and delicious dish with game."

• • • • •

How to Cook Long-Grain Rice

Several of my game recipes say "serve over a bed of rice." However, I haven't followed the rice box's cooking directions for a couple of years—not since I complimented a friend on her rice and asked what brand she used. It was the same as mine, but she let me in on her secret. She grew up in Trinidad where they cook rice in *lots of water* and then drain and wash it. The cooked rice is light, fluffy, and completely starch-free.

In a large saucepan, boil at least 3 cups of water, lightly salted. Add ⅔ cup rice (for 4 servings), cover tightly, and simmer for 20 minutes, until it is tender to the bite. Pour the rice into a strainer or colander to drain, and rinse well under hot running water. Drain *thoroughly* and pour back into the saucepan. Add 2 tablespoons of butter and toss with a fork over medium heat until the rice is well coated with butter and piping hot. Serve immediately. 4 servings.

• • • • •

Creole Rice

> ½ cup chopped onion
> ½ cup chopped celery with leaves
> ½ cup chopped green pepper
> 1 pint (16 ounces) canned tomatoes and juice
> 1 tablespoon parsley flakes (or chopped parsley)
> 1 bay leaf
> 3 dashes Tabasco sauce
> ½ cup uncooked long-grain rice
> Salt & pepper

Place the onion, celery, green pepper, and parsley in a saucepan. Squeeze the liquid lightly from the canned tomatoes into a measuring cup and add enough water to the liquid to measure 1¼ cups. Add the tomatoes and the liquid to the saucepan along with the Tabasco sauce and bay leaf. Add a little salt and pepper. Heat the vegetables until they are at the boiling point and add rice. Butter an oven-proof casserole and pour the rice/vegetable mixture into it. Cover with a lid or foil and bake in a preheated 350°F. oven for 45 minutes. Discard bay leaf and serve. Serves 4.

Tip: If you are using the broiler for the main dish, cook the dish before time to broil and leave it in the bottom of the oven to keep warm until dinner.

Note: "Especially good with waterfowl."

• • • • •

Wild Rice & Mushrooms

> ⅔ cup wild rice
> 1 cup sliced fresh mushrooms
> 4 tablespoons butter
> Salt & pepper
> 2 tablespoons chopped fresh parsley

Wash the rice in cold water and place in a saucepan with about 4 cups of hot water. Bring to a boil and simmer, covered, until plump and tender—about 35 minutes. Don't overcook or it will be mushy.

While the rice is cooking, heat the butter in a large skillet and fry the mushroom slices over medium-high heat until brown, about 7 minutes. When the rice is tender, drain in a strainer and rinse under hot, running water. *Drain well* and add to the mushrooms. Stir and heat until all are piping hot. Serve immediately. Serves 4.

Note: "Excellent side dish for all game."

• • • • •

Elegant Wild Rice Casserole

> ½ cup uncooked wild rice
> 3 tablespoons butter
> ¼ cup pine nuts or slivered almonds
> 2 tablespoons minced green onions
> ½ cup chopped mushrooms
> 2 chicken bouillon cubes
> 1½ cups hot water

Wash the rice in cold water and drain. Melt the butter in a skillet and add rice, pine nuts, green onions, and mushrooms. Fry over medium-high heat for about 7 minutes. Add bouillon cubes and water and heat to the boiling point, crushing the bouillon. Pour into a small, buttered casserole dish, cover, and place in a preheated 325°F. oven for 1½ hours. Serves 4 as a side dish (double for 8 servings).

Note: "Excellent company dish since it can be placed in the oven early."

•　•　•　•　•

How to Bake Potatoes

It sounds like a simple thing and it is. But there are a couple of things you want to avoid: new potatoes (they have too much moisture and are always soggy), and baking them in foil (you are then really steaming the potatoes—end result is soggy). Good baked potatoes should be dry and fluffy.

Select six large baking (most supermarkets label them) potatoes and scrub well, removing all bruised spots with the tip of a knife. Place in a preheated 425°F. oven and bake for 1 to 1¼ hours, depending on how big they are. Halfway through the baking, pierce each potato with a fork. This allows the steam to escape, saving the potato from exploding in the oven. Test by piercing with a table fork—when it goes in easily, they are done. Serve four of the potatoes (for four people) and save the other two for the next recipe.

Note: "Easy side dish with game that has been fried or broiled."

•　•　•　•　•

Fried Potatoes

    2 large, leftover, baked potatoes
    3 tablespoons butter
      Salt & pepper
      Onion powder

Dice the potatoes with their skins. Melt butter in a medium-size skillet and add the potatoes. Fry over medium-high heat, until brown on all sides—about 10 minutes. While frying, sprinkle with a little salt, pepper, and onion powder. Serve immediately. Serves 4.

Note: "Great dish."

• • • • •

Baked Stuffed Potatoes

>   4 large baking potatoes
>   4 slices of bacon, cut into small pieces
>   ½ cup chopped onions
>   1½ teaspoons dried dillweed
>   ¾ cup sour cream
>   1 large egg, beaten

Scrub potatoes and put in a preheated 425°F. oven. Bake them for 1 to 1¼ hours until fork pierces them easily. Halfway through the baking, pierce them with a fork.

Fry the bacon in a small skillet over medium-high heat until the bacon is crisp. Remove it with a slotted spoon and allow it to drain on paper towels. Add onion to the skillet and cook for 5 minutes until tender.

When the potatoes are done, cut a lengthwise slice out of the top of each potato and spoon the insides out into a bowl. Mash the potato pulp and add the bacon, onion, dillweed, sour cream, and beaten egg to the bowl. Using a beater, whip the potatoes until thoroughly mixed. Mound the potato mixture back into the shells. (At this point the potatoes can be held at room temperature for up to an hour, or refrigerated for a couple hours.) Bake the stuffed potatoes on a baking sheet in a preheated 425°F. oven for 10 minutes if they are at room temperature (20 minutes if they are cold). Serves 4.

Note: "Jim's favorite stuffed potato recipe; they go well with all game."

• • • • •

Potatoes Rosemary

2 pounds red-skinned potatoes (small ones are best)
⅓ cup peanut oil
1 teaspoon salt
½ teaspoon rosemary leaves, crushed

Crush the rosemary on a wooden board with the back of a wooden spoon. Scrub potatoes (but don't peel) and cut into ⅛-inch slices. (The potatoes can be held at this point for an hour by covering with cold water. Dry *thoroughly* on paper towels before proceeding with the recipe.) In a bowl, combine the potatoes with the oil, salt, and crushed rosemary. Spread the slices out on the bottom of a 13-by-9-inch baking dish. Cover with foil tightly and bake in a preheated 350°F. oven for 30 minutes. Remove foil, turn the potatoes over, and bake another 20 minutes (uncovered) until tender. Serves 6.

Note: "Delicious."

• • • • •

Potato Salad

4 medium-size potatoes
½ cup chopped celery
2 tablespoons finely chopped green onion
½ cup sliced fresh mushrooms (optional)
1 hard-boiled egg, sliced
½ cup mayonnaise
1½ tablespoons Dijon-style mustard
2 teaspoons horseradish
¼ teaspoon tarragon
Salt & pepper

Mix the dressing by combining the mayonnaise, mustard, horseradish, and tarragon. Cover and refrigerate for at least 3 hours to marry the flavors.

Scrub the potatoes and boil, covered with water, until fork-tender, about 30 minutes. (Time depends on the size of the potatoes.) Drain and allow the potatoes to cool thoroughly, then peel and dice. Put the potatoes, celery, green onions, and mushrooms in a large bowl. Add the dressing and toss gently until well blended. If desired, more mayonnaise may be added. Top the dish with sliced egg and sprinkle with salt and pepper. Serves 4 to 6.

Note: "Good dish for outside meal."

• • • • •

Fruit and Ice Cream

> 2 cups bite-size chunks or slices of fresh fruit
> (strawberries, peaches, or pineapple)
> Sugar
> 3 tablespoons Madeira wine

Put the cut fruit in a bowl and toss gently with just enough sugar to cut the tartness. The amount will vary depending on the fruit. I use about ¼ cup with strawberries. Stir in the Madeira, cover the dish, and allow to set at room temperature for 1 hour. Occasionally turn the fruit over from top to bottom to blend the flavors. Serve ladled generously over vanilla ice cream. Serves 4 to 6.

Note: "Perfect ending to a game dinner."

• • • • •

Brandied Apples

> 2 large cooking apples, peeled and thinly sliced
> 2 tablespoons butter
> 1 teaspoon lemon rind
> ¼ cup sugar
> ¼ cup sour cream
> 2 tablespoons brandy

Melt the butter in a large, heavy skillet. Add the apple slices (Northern Spy is best, or a good cooking apple like Granny Smith) and lemon rind and stir to coat with butter. Turn heat to high and add the sugar and cream. Time the apples from this point for about 3 minutes. Stir well and add the brandy. Mix constantly until the apples are limp but still a little crisp. Cool slightly and serve as is or over vanilla ice cream. Serves 4.

Note: "Super ending to a game meal."

•   •   •   •   •

The Wise Surprise

      3 snack-size Hershey Krackel bars
      1 tablespoon chocolate syrup
      2 shots brandy
      1½ to 2 cups (1 pint) vanilla ice cream

This delicious combination dessert/after dinner drink was invented with leftover Halloween candy, hence the small Krackel bars.

In a blender, place candy bars, chocolate syrup, brandy, and ice cream. Mix well and serve in brandy or wine glasses. Will serve two. Double for four servings. If you wish to make more, make in two batches. (The recipe was named for friend Jack Wise who insisted that it be included in this book after tasting it.)

Note: "Super."

•   •   •   •   •

Index